*Quantitative Analysis of
Computer Systems*

Quantitative Analysis of Computer Systems

Clement H. C. Leung

Computer Science Department,
Birkbeck College,
University of London.

JOHN WILEY & SONS

Chichester · New York · Brisbane · Toronto · Singapore

Library of Congress Cataloging-in-Publication Data:

Leung, Clement H. C.
  Quantitative analysis of computer systems.
  Bibliography: p.
  1. Electronic digital computers—Evaluation.
I. Title.   II. Series.
QA76.9.E94L48   1987   004.2′4   87-2046
ISBN 0 471 91509 2
ISBN 0 471 91508 4 (pbk.)

Printed and bound in Great Britain by Biddles Ltd, Guildford

To Qui Hoon, Timothy,
and My Parents

*'Unless the Lord builds the house,
those who build it labour in vain.'*
Psalms 127, Verse 1.

Contents

Preface xi

1 The Purpose of Quantitative Analysis 1

   1.1   Introduction 1
   1.2   Analytic Models 1
   1.3   Simulation Models 2
   1.4   Comparison of Analytic and Simulation Models 3
   1.5   Prediction and Measurement 4
   1.6   Tuning and Optimization 4

2 The Nature of Computer Systems Events and Their Descriptions . 6

   2.1   Descriptions of Uncertainty: Histograms, Frequency Functions
        and Cumulative Distribution Functions 6
   2.2   Mean, Variance, and Coefficient of Variation 10
   2.3   Examples 12
   2.4   Point Events in Computer Systems 16
       2.4.1   The Point Description 17
       2.4.2   The Interval Description 18
       2.4.3   Operations on Poisson Streams: Merging and Splitting . . 20
       2.4.4   The Importance of the Poisson Process 22
   2.5   Summary 23
   2.6   Exercises 23

3 Resource Contention: Basic Parameters and Measures of Effectiveness 26

   3.1   Basic Structure of a Queueing System 26
       3.1.1   The Request Arrival Characteristics 26
       3.1.2   The Service Requirement and Departure Characteristics 27
       3.1.3   The Service Capacity 27
       3.1.4   The Scheduling Rule 28
   3.2   A Shorthand Notation for the Specification of a Queueing System 28
   3.3   Work, Traffic Intensity, Utilization, and Throughput 29
   3.4   Measures of Effectiveness 32
       3.4.1   User-oriented Measures 32
       3.4.2   System-oriented Measures 32
   3.5   Summary 33
   3.6   Exercises 33

4 Fundamental Relationships and Their Applications 35

   4.1   Relationships Between Delay and Queue Size: Little's Formulae 35

4.2   The Mean Response Time 36
   4.2.1   The Pollaczek–Khintchine Formulae 37
   4.2.2   The Generalized Pollaczek–Khintchine Formulae . . . 40
4.3   Classification of Arrival Characteristics 42
4.4   Classification of Service Characteristics 43
4.5   A Reliable Operating Environment: Conservative Systems . . 44
4.6   Summary 45
4.7   Appendix 4A: The Mean Residual Service Delay Relating to
   Pollaczek–Khintchine Formula 46
4.8   Appendix 4B: The Mean Residual Service Delay Relating to
   the Generalized Pollaczek–Khintchine formula 47
4.9   Exercises 47

5   Systems with Service Discriminations **50**

5.1   Introduction 50
5.2   Non-preemptive Priority Systems 50
   5.2.1   The Mean Waiting Time 51
   5.2.2   Invariance Property 54
   5.2.3   Optimal Priority Assignment 56
5.3   Preemptive Resume Priority Systems 57
5.4   The Shortest-job-first Rule 59
5.5   The Round-robin Rule 62
5.6   The Processor Sharing Rule 63
5.7   Summary 65
5.8   Appendix 5A: The Average Unfinished Work 66
5.9   Exercises 67

6   Systems with Practical Limitations **70**

6.1   Introduction 70
6.2   The Number of Jobs in the System 70
6.3   The System M/M/1 72
6.4   The System M/M/1 With Limited Buffer 73
6.5   The System M/M/1 With Finite Population: The Interactive
   Response Time Formula 75
6.6   The M/M/m Loss System: Erlang's B Formula 77
6.7   The System M/M/m: Erlang's C Formula 77
6.8   The System M/M/∞ 79
6.9   Summary 79
6.10 Exercises 80

7   Networks of Queues **81**

7.1   Introduction 81
7.2   The Output of a M/M/m Queue: Burke's Theorem 82
7.3   Feedforward Networks 83

7.4 General Exponential Open Queueing Networks: Jackson's
Theorem 85
7.5 Closed Queueing Networks 90
7.6 Summary 91
7.7 Exercises 92

8 Operational Analysis 94
8.1 Introduction 94
8.2 Fundamental Operational Laws and Theorems 94
8.3 Queueing Networks 97
8.4 Bottleneck Analysis for Closed Queueing Networks 100
8.5 Summary 103
8.6 Exercises 103

9 Database and I/O Subsystem Performance 105
9.1 Introduction 105
9.2 Basic Storage Structures 106
9.3 The Fixed Head Disk 106
9.3.1 The FIFO Fixed Head Disk with Variable Length Records 106
9.3.2 The FIFO Fixed Head Disk with Fixed Length Records . 107
9.3.3 The SLTF Fixed Head Disk with Fixed Length Records . 108
9.3.4 The SLTF Fixed Head Disk with Variable Length Records 109
9.4 The Movable Head Disk 109
9.4.1 The Random Seek Distribution 109
9.4.2 The FIFO Disk with Variable Length Records 110
9.4.3 The SCAN Disk with Variable Length Records 111
9.4.4 The FIFO Disk with Fixed Length Records 111
9.5 File Buffering and Locality Referencing 112
9.6 Models of Database Reorganization 114
9.7 Summary 117
9.8 Exercises 117

10 Approximations and Time-dependent System Behaviour 119
10.1 Introduction 119
10.2 The Equilibrium Waiting Time and Queue Size of the $G/G/1$
System: Diffusion Approximation 120
10.3 Time-dependent Behaviour of $G/G/1$ 121
10.4 Heavy Traffic Approximation for the $G/G/m$ System . . . 122
10.5 Summary 122
10.6 Exercises 122

11 Workload Modelling and Characterization 124
11.1 Introduction 124
11.2 Benchmarks 125

11.3   Synthetic Jobs 125
11.4   Kernels 126
11.5   Scripts 126
11.6   Instruction Mixes 127
11.7   Measure of Computing Power 129
11.8   Summary. 130
11.9   Exercises. 131

12   Performance Measurement and Monitoring **132**
12.1   Introduction. 132
12.2   Hardware Monitors 132
12.3   Software Monitors. 133
12.4   Firmware and Hybrid Monitors 135
12.5   Presentation and Interpretation of Measurement Results . . 136
       12.5.1   Gantt Charts 136
       12.5.2   Kiviat Graphs 137
12.6   Summary. 141
12.7   Exercises. 141

13   Performance Tuning and Improvement **142**
13.1   Introduction. 142
13.2   General System Tuning 142
13.3   Program Behaviour and Execution Efficiency 145
13.4   Load Balancing and Optimization 147
13.5   Summary. 149
13.6   Exercises. 149

14   System Simulation **151**
14.1   Introduction. 151
14.2   Random Number Generation 154
14.3   Generation of Continuous Non-uniform Random Numbers 156
       14.3.1   Inverse Transform Method 156
       14.3.2   Rejection Method 157
       14.3.3   Generation of Normally Distributed Random Numbers 158
14.4   Simulation Programming 158
14.5   Summary. 160
14.6   Exercises. 160

Bibliography **162**

Index **166**

Preface

Quantitative computer performance analysis consists of discovering and ascertaining the efficiency of a computer system; it may be, for example, concerned with the estimation of the performance behaviour of systems under construction, or monitoring that of an existing one. The findings of a quantitative performance study may be used to guide decisions relating to system design, the allocation of machine resources, the acquisition of additional facilities, or the tuning of an existing configuration. Carrying out proper performance analysis is recognized to be an integral part of the professional construction and management of computer systems. The pervasiveness of such an essential function means that the associated method is an indispensable and practical tool with which every system designer should be equipped.

This book presents a body of *proven* methods established over the years on quantitative performance analysis and is mostly based on course materials given to computer science students at Reading and London Universities. The knowledge of computing assumed of the students is basic operating systems, machine architecture, and data structures. Admittedly, there already exist a number of books written on the subject, but most of them, ironically, seem to have more appeal to students of mathematics and statistics than to those of computer science. As a result, a large proportion of computer science students are uneasy about quantitative computer systems analysis because they either find the whole subject obscure and difficult to understand, or find it difficult to relate the sometimes excessively theoretical treatment to concrete performance situations. There is little doubt that computer science students tend to view performance analysis as a practical discipline which can be applied to real-life situations, and thus they often prefer to rely on physical insight and intuition rather than on formal arguments. This book is written primarily, though not exclusively, with such students in mind, and the emphasis here is on practical applications and usable results rather than on the general techniques of analysis. In addition, the applied character of the book will also appeal to practitioners, and it will furnish a useful reference for systems analysts and software engineers. It does not mean, however, that the reader is simply stuffed with a host of formulae without due explanation given concerning their meaning and validity; nor does it mean that a diluted treatment of performance analysis is presented with everything except results of the simplest kind filtered off, leaving the reader with limited confidence in the subject. On the contrary, it is felt that confidence is best fostered by frequent appeals to intuition and by building from a simple and familiar mathematical framework. The mathematics used in this book is at a level with which most students of computer science are completely at ease, assuming a no more than a working knowledge of elementary calculus and basic probability. The author believes that a detailed familiarity with applied probability theory and stochastic processes, though obviously an asset, is not strictly essential to gaining a thorough understanding of quantitative computer performance analysis, and is in any case asking too much of the majority of the computer science students and readers. The author has found that, even though a student may have taken university courses on probability theory and statistics before, often in their first year, it is rarely safe to assume that he or she always retains a clear mastery of all the materials taught in those courses; accordingly, even concepts such as frequency function, mean, and coefficient of variation are carefully reviewed and explained at the beginning of the book. Whenever feasible, elaborate mathematical manipulations are replaced by intuitively plausible arguments—a good example being provided by Little's formula—and in cases where a more convincing mathematical proof is considered unavoidable, it is either relegated to the appendix of the appropriate chapters, or for highly involved ones, the reader is directed to the relevant references. In this way, the risk of losing sight of the physical meaning of the results is minimized but, at the same time, the reader's confidence in them is not undermined. At the end of every chapter, a summary of the key results and concepts treated is given, and throughout the text numerous illustrative examples are provided.

The materials in this book may be broadly divided into three parts. The first part, consisting of Chapters 1–3, gives the background and motivation of quantitative performance analysis; the second part, consisting of Chapters 4–10, deals with the prediction and modelling of system efficiency through analytic descriptions; the final part, consisting of Chapters 11–14, deals primarily with the empirical approaches relating to performance tuning and monitoring. Apart from being suitable as a self-contained text on computer performance analysis, this book can also be used as a supplementary text for other computer science courses in which some degree of quantitative analysis is called for; indeed, materials in this book have been used by the author in courses on database systems, computer networks, and operating systems.

There are a number of useful topics treated in this book which are not normally considered to be standard in a first course on performance analysis. Here, apart from the conventional Pollaczek–Khintchine formula, a useful generalization of it in which busy period initiators are allowed to possess different service characteristics from those of other requests is covered in detail. This simple generalization is especially valuable for analyzing facilities which require additional set-up time when starting from 'cold', and it also represents a more natural approach in capturing the salient characteristics of certain I/O (input/output) devices. There is a separate chapter exclusively devoted to the study of database and I/O subsystem efficiency, partly because database accesses are almost always unavoidable in most present day systems, and partly because—due to their slow mechanical nature—disk databases are likely sources of performance bottleneck. Owing to their practical importance, there is also a separate chapter on approximations and time-dependent behaviour. In addition, the analysis of queueing networks using the powerful yet simple method of operational analysis—which does not seem to be widely available in book form—is treated in detail.

CHAPTER 1

The Purpose of Quantitative Analysis

1.1 Introduction

In designing and building complex systems with a large number of interacting components—whether computer, engineering, or industrial systems—it is always necessary to ascertain the effectiveness of a design. Apart from building a system that fulfils the prescribed functions, it is often essential to determine the behaviour and efficiency of the system in a *quantitative* manner.

Consider an everyday example: a road traffic system. It is irresponsible and unprofessional for a designer just to propose a particular road configuration making use of components such as roundabouts, traffic lights, zebra crossings etc. without saying something about the likelihood and magnitude of traffic jams and possible delays, since these are quantities of primary interest to the road users as well as the transportation planners. The efficiency of the system, as measured by the traffic delays in this case, will require a quantitative analysis of system behaviour.

Similarly in computer systems, simply to build one without saying something about its effectiveness and efficiency in a quantitative way could have serious consequences. For instance, building a real-time system that is subsequently found to have an unacceptably poor response time may defeat the purpose of the project and discredit the entire system altogether. In order to study a system quantitatively, it is essential to place it in a suitable context by adopting a set of assumptions before proceeding with the analysis; in other words, one needs to make use of an appropriate model to represent the system. Two types of models are common in quantitative systems analysis: analytic and simulation models. These are discussed in the following two sections.

1.2 Analytic Models

An analytic model makes use of a set of equations to describe system behaviour and to derive mathematically the performance characteristics of the system. The solutions of an analytic model may be exact or approximate, but they invariably represent the results of a mathematical analysis. An exact solution is the result of a precise analysis of a given situation based on a set of model assumptions. Although the assumptions may only be approximately true for the situation in question, the solutions nevertheless are exact given the agreed

1

set of assumptions. An approximate solution, on the other hand, relates to an imprecise analysis of a situation. Although, in principle, it is possible to have an exact solution to the problem, it is either impractical or impossible to discover these solutions due to mathematical intractability. The approximate solutions, in general, are different from the corresponding exact solutions—although they may coincide in special cases—and such differences may be sufficiently small under certain conditions, so that the approximate solutions are nevertheless able to provide valuable indications of system behaviour.

In analytic studies, one can adopt either a deterministic or a probabilistic approach. The former implies that system parameters and their interactions can be known with certainty and that external influences can be accounted for precisely. This approach is, of course, not always realistic as chance elements are frequently present in real-life situations and their effect is often significant; for example, in processing a database transaction, one can never predict exactly what the response time would be as it depends on other jobs running on the computer system at the time, the degree of multiprogramming, the number of disk accesses required for the transaction, and the prevailing communication line traffic. Hence a probabilistic model, which takes into account the random elements of a situation, should be a more faithful and accurate representation of reality. Admittedly, a probabilistic approach generally increases the complexity of the analysis and this may sometimes defeat the purpose of analytic studies as the problem could, as a result, become intractable. Under such circumstances, simplifying assumptions may have to be made to keep the problem tractable but, at the same time, without introducing unacceptable distortion into the model. In a situation where chance influence is dominant, a probabilistic approach provides a better approximation to reality than a purely deterministic one, and in such a context the probabilistic approach can be regarded as an essential improvement over the basic deterministic approach.

As indicated earlier, to study a system analytically, first of all one must adopt a set of assumptions. Certain assumptions may lead to elegant exact solutions while others may only lead to cumbersome or approximate solutions. In the process of selecting the assumptions, one is often engaged in making an approximation nevertheless because different assumptions tend to describe reality in varying degrees of accuracy. Thus approximations may be introduced in two stages: during model specification and during analysis. The inaccuracies introduced in the former tend to be rather difficult to quantify, while those of the latter may be ascertained in more precise mathematical terms.

1.3 Simulation Models

A simulation model consists of capturing the characteristics of the system and representing them by means of a suite of computer programs. By running these programs, the dynamic behaviour of the system is acted out, so that by collecting suitable data on the computer model of the system—as captured by these programs—it is possible to say something about the performance of the actual system. Conceptually, a simulation study is similar to carrying out a measurement experiment except that these measurements are taken on a computer model of the system rather than on the actual system, and that these measurements are always reproducible. A simulation study has a number of advantages over direct measurement:

- any extraneous factors irrelevant to the present experimental objectives may be excluded,
- any noise in the data may be filtered off,
- the observation period may be much longer than for a real system,
- no interference to actual system operation is produced.

Like analytic models, however, a set of assumptions is always necessary for a simulation model. A detailed comparison between analytic and simulation models is given in the next section.

1.4 Comparison of Analytic and Simulation Models

The principal advantage of a simulation model over an analytic model is that the former allows the incorporation of many more details, which are often difficult to explicitly include in an analytic model. In addition, more flexible assumptions may be adopted in a simulation model without affecting the production of results: if these flexible assumptions were adopted in an analytic model, the problem may become unsolvable as a result. It is generally true that any numerical results which can be obtained by analytic means can always be produced by simulation but not vice versa.

Simulation models, however, are both expensive in development cost—programming, debugging, and validation—and in running cost, especially when equilibrium operating conditions need to be observed. Nor does a simulation model permit much sensitivity analysis and extrapolation from a given set of experimental conditions, since a change in a single parameter of the model usually means re-running the entire simulation. In particular, establishing upper and lower bounds on system performance, and demonstrating the optimality of algorithms and procedures are not normally possible with a simulation model. It is fair to say that simulation models are primarily empirical in character, and their results admit only limited interpretation. Analytic models, on the other hand, though they cannot perhaps accommodate as many details as simulation ones, offer a relatively inexpensive alternative for evaluating system performance as well as permitting conclusions to be drawn respecting the causal relationships among system parameters.

Very often, a combination of both approaches is useful. Even if one ultimately decides to gauge the performance of different alternatives by means of detailed simulation modelling, analytic studies can nevertheless help to eliminate at the outset those which are clearly undesirable, thereby reducing the number of simulation models which need to be finally built. In addition, a complete model of a system may make use of both approaches: certain subsystems may be represented analytically interfacing with others which are based on simulation. This kind of *hybrid model* will reduce the overall cost of model construction as well as the running cost.

1.5 Prediction and Measurement

There are many reasons for studying the efficiency of a system. For example, in system design one may wish to compare the desirability of a number of alternatives; or in the case of operational systems, one may have detected deficiencies and wanted to find out where and how they are caused. Where the system under study is not yet available, one is undertaking a *predictive evaluation*. In so doing one has to rely on suitable representations of the system—usually in terms of analytic or simulation models—in order to derive results concerning system behaviour. By suitably interpreting these results, meaningful estimates of system performance may be formed. Where the system under study already exists, then it is possible to carry out measurements on it. Since taking measurements is generally expensive—typically necessitating the availability and setting up of a *hardware monitor* or a *software monitor*—as well as interfering with existing system operation, it needs to be carefully planned out. When a number of effects need to be studied, the measurement period may be very lengthy in order to isolate them properly. As measurement is primarily geared to existing configurations and workload, projection into the future is not directly possible. However, it has the key advantage of working with the actual system rather than a model of it; this will eliminate any inaccuracies introduced by the modelling process.

1.6 Tuning and Optimization

Performance optimization means that by suitably adjusting the configuration and parameters of a system, it is possible to get the best performance out of it according to some criterion. In most cases, performance optimization undertakings do not involve the upgrading of hardware components; since having faster hardware almost always gives rise to better performance, performance optimization achieved primarily through hardware upgrade seems rather too simple and uninteresting.

In analytic modelling, optimization may involve the use of techniques such as mathematical programming, the differentiation of mathematical expressions to determine the optimal parameter setting, or systematically searching a given solution space to obtain the best solution.

Performance tuning is a kind of optimization carried out on an existing system. By taking measurements and analyzing them, it is possible to determine where the inefficiencies lie; by reducing the effect of or eliminating these inefficiencies, it is possible to produce a more efficient system. The result of performance tuning is to introduce improvement to the system, but since tuning is largely empirical in character, it obviously cannot be relied on to produce the best solution in the mathematical sense. It is frequently true that the ultimate objective in conducting measurement experiments is to be able to carry out meaningful performance tuning on the system under study.

CHAPTER 2

The Nature of Computer Systems Events and Their Descriptions

2.1 Descriptions of Uncertainty: Histograms, Frequency Functions and Cumulative Distribution Functions

Due to the complex interaction between a large number of components and processes within the computer system, the durations and occurrences of events there cannot normally be predicted exactly. The uncertainty resulting from such complex interaction, although random in nature, do tend to conform to prescribed patterns, and by examining the collective behaviour, it is quite possible to meaningfully predict behaviour in individual cases. For example, consider the execution time X (measured in minutes) of a particular job, and suppose the following data have been collected for 8 runs: 10.7, 11.3, 10.2, 9.6, 8.8, 10.1, 9.8, 10.6. Although it is admittedly not possible to ascertain from these differing data values the precise execution time of any given run, it does not mean that nothing meaningful can be said concerning the duration of its execution. From the data values, one may nevertheless infer that the execution time of that particular job, although it exhibits some variation, is roughly 10 minutes; or even more informatively, we may say that the execution time is 10 ± 2 minutes—meaning that we are reasonably confident that its variable execution time lies between the limits 8 and 12 minutes. All these are meaningful statements which convey useful information about the execution time of the job in question.

In computer performance evaluation, one cannot in general make exact statements about a given situation, but instead one frequently has to be content with *probability statements*. With a probability statement, one is not one hundred percent certain about the facts being asserted, but instead one attaches a percentage expressing one's confidence or certainty about the validity of the statement. Probability statements are generally based either on observation of past behaviour or on assumptions concerning the operational characteristics of the situation. Evidently, when one bases a probability statement on past observations, one's certainty of the statement generally improves with increased samples. However, when a vast amount of observational data has been accumulated, the mass of raw data in unprocessed form is of limited value, and it is through appropriately summarizing and displaying them that they are converted into an intelligible and useful form. Consider

6

Table 2.1 Execution time data

Execution time (min)	Absolute frequency	Relative frequency (%)	Cumulative frequency (%)
(8, 9]	1	12.5	12.5
(9, 10]	2	25.0	37.5
(10, 11]	4	50.0	87.5
(11, 12]	1	12.5	100.0

again the execution time data above, and suppose we wish to display them graphically. First we group them into five classes of one minute interval each as in Table 2.1; the interval notation $(a, b]$ signifies the set of values v for which $a < v \leqslant b$. The values in the appropriate columns are obtained as follows: column 2, the absolute frequency, gives the actual count of the number of jobs falling into the appropriate classes; column 3, the relative frequency, expresses the appropriate count as a percentage of the total; column 4, the cumulative frequency, is obtained by adding the relative frequencies of all preceding classes to that of the class in question. Fig. 2.1 plots the relative

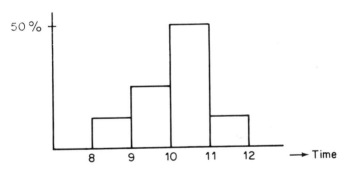

FIGURE 2.1.   Frequency histogram

frequency using this grouping which is often called a *histogram*. From such a presentation, one could immediately make a number of informative statements about the variable execution time of the job. For example, we see that only for 12.5% of the time, the execution time actually exceeds 11 minutes, and that half of the time it lies between 10 and 11 minutes. We also note that in this example, the sum of the total areas of the rectangles is one. In fact, a histogram offers a useful and relatively complete description of the uncertainty associated with a situation, and it conveys so much meaningful information that it is always convenient to express uncertainty in terms of histograms. In this example, we have 'coarsened' the data values by grouping them into

8

classes; obviously we can increase the resolution by suitably reducing the class width and increasing the number of classes, and so conveying even more detailed and accurate information on the variable job execution time. If we conceptually shrink the class width to an extremely small value while keeping the total areas of the rectangles equal to one, then we obtain a mathematical idealization called a *frequency function* which, in the case of a continuous

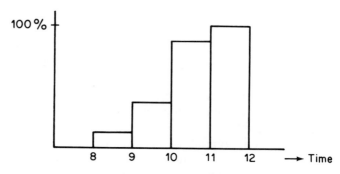

FIGURE 2.2.   Cumulative frequency

random quantity, is more commonly referred to as a *probability density function*. From a probability density function $f(x)$ we can make probability statements in much the same way as from a histogram of observational data. For example, the probability that the job execution time of a particular run lies between a and b, $\Pr[a < X < b]$, is obtained by summing the appropriate relative frequencies and is given by the area under the curve $f(x)$ between these limits; in symbols, this is

$$\Pr[a < X < b] = \int_a^b f(x)\,\mathrm{d}x.$$

The integrand $f(x)\,\mathrm{d}x$ may be viewed as an infinitesimal rectangle in the corresponding histogram, and roughly gives the probability of occurrence of the value x. Of course, the percentage of jobs with execution time lying between zero and infinity is one hundred by definition of the relative frequency.

Apart from the frequency histogram representation, sometimes it is useful to consider the cumulative frequency. The cumulative frequency of the job execution data using the above grouping is plotted in Fig. 2.2; from it, we can answer questions such as the probability that the execution time of a given run does not exceed a given value. The corresponding mathematical idealization of the cumulative frequency is the *cumulative distribution function*; for a cumulative distribution function $F(x)$, its value at the point x is the total area to the left of x under the corresponding frequency function $f(x)$; i.e.

$$F(x) = \int_0^x f(u) \, du,$$

which gives the probability that the associated variable quantity does not exceed the value x; similarly, the probability that the quantity does not fall below the value x is $1 - F(x)$, which is often referred to as the *complementary distribution function*. It is evident that the frequency function $f(x)$ can be obtained from the cumulative distribution function $F(x)$ by differentiation; i.e. $f(x) = F'(x)$. The cumulative distribution function also provides a complete description of uncertainty, and from it one can, in fact, make probability statements even simpler than from a frequency function; for example, the probability that the job execution time lies between a and b can be read off more or less directly from the cumulative distribution function without recourse to integration (which may be laborious at times); i.e. $\Pr[a < X < b] = F(b) - F(a)$. The frequency function and the cumulative distribution function provide alternative, but equivalent, specifications of the characteristics of a random quantity since knowing either of them allows the other to be determined.

So far, we have been mainly concerned with continuous quantities of which job execution time is an example. In computer systems, we also frequently encounter discrete variable quantities such as the number of jobs submitted in a given day or the number of users logged on at a given time. In such cases, the corresponding frequency function is called a *probability mass function*, which is the discrete counterpart of the probability density function. A probability mass function is a function $p(x)$ where the argument x ranges over a given set S of discrete—typically integral—values, so that the sum of $p(x)$ over all x belonging to S always equals one. For example, suppose we are interested in the variable number of jobs N submitted in a day and that, from past data, it is known to have probability mass function $p(x)$. Here, the set S could be taken to be the set of nonnegative integers, and the probability $\Pr[40 < N < 50]$ that there are between 40 and 50 jobs submitted, for example, would be

$$\Pr[40 < N < 50] = \sum_{40 < x < 50} p(x).$$

Likewise, the corresponding cumulative distribution function $P(y)$, similarly to that in the continuous case, is

$$P(y) = \sum_{x < y} p(x),$$

which gives the probability that the number of jobs submitted is less than y.

In this book, when there is no ambiguity, frequency function will be used to signify either probability density function or probability mass function, and the term distribution will be used to denote either frequency function or cumulative distribution function. When a random quantity conforms to a certain distribution, say $g(x)$, we often say that it obeys the *distribution law* $g(x)$.

2.2 Mean, Variance, and Coefficient of Variation

Although quite detailed and informative probability statements could be made from the frequency function or the cumulative distribution function, frequently these are not available owing to the complexity of the situation. As a practical necessity, one would therefore have to be content with simple numerical measures which, to some extent, summarize the salient features of the distribution. Although the information conveyed by these numerical values is in general less complete, but because they are ordinary numbers rather than functions, they prove to be much easier to handle and manipulate, and they are often adequate for most practical purposes. The most important of such measures is the mean value: the *mean* or average of a random quantity X, denoted by $\bar{X}$, is simply the weighted combination of all the appropriate values with respect to its frequency function; i.e.

$$\bar{X} = \begin{cases} \int xf(x)\,dx, & \text{if } X \text{ is continuous with} \\ & \text{probability density function } f(x), \\ \Sigma\, xp(x), & \text{if } X \text{ is discrete with} \\ & \text{probability mass function } p(x), \end{cases} \tag{2.2.1}$$

where the integration/summation is taken over the entire range of values the quantity may assume. If we imagine that the probability density function signifies the density of a rod of unit mass lying along the x-axis, then the mean gives its centre of mass, and it furnishes a measure of the central or typical value of the variable quantity. More generally, the average of an arbitrary expression $h(X)$ involving a random quantity X is defined, for continuous X with probability density function $f(x)$, as

$$\overline{h(X)} = \int h(x)f(x)\,dx.$$

The case for a discrete quantity is analogously defined using the probability mass function. It is evident from the above definition that, for any constant c, we have in general

$$\overline{cX} = c\bar{X}. \tag{2.2.2}$$

In the special case that a random quantity turns out to be a constant—which is called a *deterministic* or *degenerate* random quantity—there is, of course, no variation present and its average simply equals the constant itself. For an expression involving two or more *independent* random quantities—i.e. the outcome of any one of them has no influence on the others—its average is obtained by averaging over all the individual quantities, one after another, using the appropriate frequency functions. For example, the average of an expression $h(X, Y)$ involving two independent quantities X and Y with respective probability mass functions $p(x)$ and $q(y)$ is

$$\overline{h(X, Y)} = \sum_y \left[\sum_x h(x, y)p(x) \right] q(y).$$

Apart from the mean, the second most important summary of a distribution is the *variance* (often abbreviated as Var) which measures the average squared deviation of the variable quantity from the mean, and is defined as

$$\text{Var}(X) = \overline{(X - \bar{X})^2},$$

which on expansion can be written as

$$\text{Var}(X) = \overline{X^2} - (\bar{X})^2. \tag{2.2.3}$$

The variance is a rough measure of the spread or dispersion of the frequency function and provides an indication as to the representativeness of the mean value: if the variance is small, then most of the values are concentrated near the mean and the latter is therefore a representative typical value; if the opposite is true, then this means that a fair proportion of the values are scattered some distance away from the mean, and so the latter is not a very representative typical value. In the case of a degenerate quantity, no variation is present and its variance is simply zero. From its definition, it is not difficult to verify that, for any constant c

$$\text{Var}(cX) = c^2 \, \text{Var}(X). \tag{2.2.4}$$

The relations (2.2.2) and (2.2.4) are often used when the variable quantity undergoes a change of unit. The term *nth moment* of a random quantity X is often used to signify the average

$$\overline{X^n};$$

from (2.2.3), we see that the variance is completely determined by the first two moments. The *standard deviation* (often abbreviated as s.d.) of a quantity is the square root of the variance and admits a similar interpretation. The standard deviation is measured in the same unit as the mean; for example, if the mean is measured in units of length, then so is the standard deviation, but the variance—involving the square of the quantity—is measured in units of area. A key property of both the mean and the variance is that of *additivity*: for two independent quantities X and Y, we have

$$\overline{X + Y} = \bar{X} + \bar{Y},$$

and

$$\text{Var}(X + Y) = \text{Var}(X) + \text{Var}(Y).$$

In fact, the additivity of the mean holds even when the quantities are not independent. The additivity of the mean and variance, of course, also applies when an arbitrary number of independent random quantities are involved. (A detailed proof of these relations is available from most texts on basic probability theory; see e.g. Feller (1968).) Sometimes, the numerical value of the standard deviation taken on its own could be misleading because its magnitude is difficult to judge without reference to that of the mean. For example, a standard deviation of 5 may be regarded as small if the mean is 1000, but is regarded as large if the mean is 10. Thus, particularly for nonnegative quantities—and in performance evaluation most of the quantities are nonnegative—it is often more meaningful to consider the relative dispersion measure $C(X)$ which expresses the standard deviation as a proportion of the mean; i.e.

$$C(X) = \text{s.d.}(X)/\bar{X}.$$

This is called the *coefficient of variation*, and is a dimensionless quantity because the units of the mean and the standard deviation, being the same, are cancelled out. As we shall see in later chapters, this is a key parameter in the performance analysis of resource contention.

2.3 Examples

The purpose of these examples is threefold: (1) to amplify the ideas introduced in the previous section; (2) to familiarize the reader with the properties of some of the common distributions which are relevant to subsequent developments; (3) to provide practical motivation as to how these distributions arise in performance evaluation.

Example 2.1 (Uniform distribution) **Basic properties**. The uniform distribution with continuous range $[a, b]$ is shown diagrammatically in Fig. 2.3; with this distribution, there is no preference value within the range and each possible value there stands equal chance of arising. In symbols, its frequency function is

$$f(x) = \begin{cases} 1/(b - a) & a \leqslant x \leqslant b \\ 0 & \text{elsewhere.} \end{cases}$$

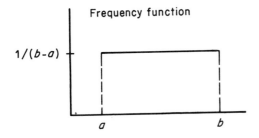

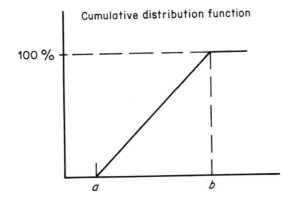

FIGURE 2.3.   The uniform distribution

The corresponding cumulative distribution function $F(x)$ is

$$F(x) = \begin{cases} 0 & x < a \\ (x - a)/(b - a) & a \leqslant x \leqslant b \\ 1 & x > b \end{cases}$$

The mean, variance, and coefficient of variation of this distribution are respectively given by

$$\text{Mean} = \int_a^b [x/(b - a)]\,dx = (a + b)/2,$$

$$\text{Variance} = \int_a^b [x - (a + b)/2]^2\,dx/(b - a) = (b - a)^2/12,$$

Coefficient of variation $= (b - a)/[(b + a)\sqrt{3}]$.

Practical motivation. The uniform distribution arises quite naturally in the evaluation of disk units. Disk units rotate at a constant speed with the read/

write head always remaining at a fixed position. Reading of data can only commence when the beginning of the required record comes under the read/write head. Depending on the position of the read/write head relative to that of the record, reading may commence immediately without delay, which would take, say, d milliseconds; in the worst case, however, a full revolution may elapse before reading can commence, which would then take $d + R$ milliseconds, where R is the duration of a full revolution. Thus, the time to read a record from such a device ranges between d and $d + R$ with all intermediate values occurring equally likely, and so obeys the uniform distribution law above with $a = d$ and $b = d + R$. $\square$

Example 2.2 (Geometric distribution) **Basic properties**. Consider a sequence of independent trials with binary outcome: success or failure, with p representing the probability of success and $q = 1 - p$ representing the probability of failure. The probability $p(k)$ that the first success occurs in the kth trial is given by the geometric probability mass function

$$p(k) = pq^{k-1}, \qquad k = 1, 2, 3 \ldots.$$

Its mean value is

$$\text{Mean} = \sum_{k>0} kp(k) = p \sum_{k>0} kq^{k-1}.$$

The last summation may be written as a derivative, i.e.

$$\text{Mean} = p \, \mathrm{d}[\sum_{k>0} q^k]/\mathrm{d}q = p \, \mathrm{d}[q/(1-q)]/\mathrm{d}q = 1/p.$$

Its variance is therefore

$$\text{Variance} = \sum_{k>0} pk^2 q^{k-1} - 1/p^2.$$

The above summation could again be evaluated by differentiation, i.e.

$$\mathrm{d}^2[\sum_{k>0} q^k]/\mathrm{d}q^2 = \sum_{k>0} k^2 q^{k-1}/q - \sum_{k>0} kq^{k-1}/q.$$

This implies that

$$\sum_{k>0} pk^2 q^{k-1} = 2q/p^2 + 1/p.$$

Substituting this into the variance expression, we obtain

$$\text{Variance} = 2q/p^2 + 1/p - 1/p^2 = q/p^2.$$

Practical motivation. In order to transfer a record from a disk unit, a data path must be established between the unit and main memory. Such a path is often provided by an I/O channel, which is normally shared among a number of devices. A common feature, called *rotational position sensing*, operates in such a way that a channel connection is only attempted when the record is ready to be transferred, i.e. when it is correctly positioned under the read/write head; if the channel is busy at that time, then a full revolution will elapse before the record again becomes correctly positioned under the read/write head, at which point another attempt to connect the channel is made. This process will be repeated until a successful connection takes place. If the probability of a successful channel connection is p, and the outcome of different connection attempts are independent, then the total delay, measured in number of disk revolutions, caused by channel blocking may be described by the geometric distribution. □

Example 2.3 (Binomial distribution) **Basic properties.** Consider again a sequence of independent trials with binary outcome as in the previous example, where p represents the probability of success, and $q = 1 - p$ represents that of a failure. Suppose here we are not interested in the variable number of trials to achieve the first success, but instead we are interested in the variable number of successes in a fixed number of trials N. The probability that there are exactly k successes occurring in prescribed positions is of course

$$p^k q^{N-k}, \qquad k = 0, 1, 2, \ldots .$$

The probability $p(k)$ of having exactly k successes without regard to position is thus the binomial distribution

$$p(k) = \binom{N}{k} p^k q^{N-k}, \qquad k = 0, 1, 2, \ldots .$$

where

$$\binom{N}{k} = N!/[k! \, (N-k)!],$$

represents the number of different ways of choosing k items out of a total of N items. The corresponding mean and variance may be obtained by applying the formulae (2.2.1) and (2.2.2). There is, however, a much simpler way of obtaining them by making use of the additivity property. Let us first consider the mean and variance of the number of success in a single trial; which are: mean $= 1 \times p + 0 \times q = p$, variance $= p(1 - p)^2 + q(0 - p)^2 = pq$. Applying the additivity of the mean and variance over the N independent trials, we conclude from the above that the mean and variance of the binomial distribution are

$$\text{Mean} = Np; \qquad \text{Variance} = Npq.$$

Practical motivation. In direct access files and hash tables, the address of an item is computed from a value associated with the item. It is by means of this computational algorithm, called the *hashing algorithm*, that items are assigned to individual address slots, each of which can hold one or more items. A desirable feature of the hashing algorithm is that it should randomize such allocations in order to produce an even distribution of items over the available address slots. A quantity of interest here is the number of items assigned to a given slot. Suppose there are N address slots and n items, and that for any

FIGURE 2.4.   Point events in time

given item assignment, each slot is picked with the same probability $1/N$. Then the probability that a given address has k items assigned to it can be viewed as having k successes out of n trials, with the probability of success equal to $1/N$. This naturally yields the binomial distribution.   □

2.4 Point Events in Computer Systems

A point event is an important type of event in computer systems. Such events are random events occurring in time; their duration is short, normally considered to be infinitesimal, and the key parameter which describes them is their time of occurrence. Examples of point events are the arrival of a job to the system, the failure of a machine component, and the initiation or termination of a process. For concreteness, we shall primarily be interpreting point events as the arrival of jobs to the system. A series of point events is represented diagrammatically in Fig. 2.4. Point events may be described by (1) the length of the time interval T separating successive points, i.e. the inter-point interval, or (2) the number of points N occurring in a given interval of time. Since T is continuous and N is discrete, point events may be specified by either a probability density function relating to T or a probability mass function relating to N. In performance evaluation, one often encounters *completely random* series of point events in which the occurrence of points in any given time interval has no bearing on that in other intervals (i.e. what happens at non-overlapping time intervals has no influence on each other). We now take a look at the properties of such completely random event series. Supposing the average number of job arrivals or point occurrences in a time interval is proportional to its length, with average rate of arrival equal to λ per unit time, then in a time interval of duration h, the average number of arrivals there is λh. If h is very small, then the number of arrivals in such an interval can only be at most one (i.e. either 0 or 1), and if p denotes the probability of an arrival there, then the average number of arrivals is approximately given by $0 \times (1 - p) + 1 \times p$. Equating this with the average number of arrivals λh, we find that the probability p of an arrival in a short interval of length h can be approximated by $p \approx \lambda h$, and such an approximation will become exact in the limit when $h \to 0$. In such a situation, we would like to obtain the properties relating to both the interval description and the point description. We shall first consider the latter; more precisely, we wish to calculate the frequency function of the number of arrivals occurring in a time interval $(0, t)$ of arbitrary length t.

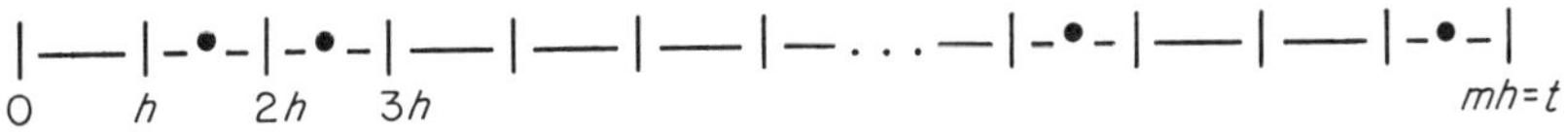

$$|\text{---}|-\bullet-|-\bullet-|\text{---}|\text{---}|\text{---}|-\cdots\text{---}|-\bullet-|\text{---}|\text{---}|-\bullet-|$$

O   h   2h   3h   mh=t

FIGURE 2.5. Partitioning the interval $(0, t)$

2.4.1 *The Point Description*

Let us partition the interval $(0, t)$ into a large number m of small subintervals each of length h as in Fig. 2.5, i.e. $h = t/m$. If h is sufficiently small, then the possibility of having more than one point occurrence in any given subinterval could be disregarded. In order to count the total number of points in $(0, t)$, we first count the number of point in each individual subinterval—which, as we have noted above, can hold at most one point—and then add them together. Each subinterval here can be regarded as an independent experimental trial with two outcomes: success with probability $p \simeq \lambda t/m$ or failure with probability $q \simeq 1 - \lambda t/m$. Thus, the probability $\Pr[N = k]$ of having precisely k points in the entire interval may be approximated by the binomial distribution:

$$\Pr[N = k] \simeq \binom{m}{k} (\lambda t/m)^k (1 - \lambda t/m)^{m-k} \qquad k = 0, 1, 2, \ldots . \quad (2.4.1)$$

Now, the right hand side of the above may be rewritten as

$$[m(m - 1) \cdots (m - k + 1)/(k! \, m^k)](\lambda t)^k (1 - \lambda t/m)^{m-k}$$

$$= [1(1 - 1/m) \cdots (1 - (k - 1)/m)/k!](\lambda t)^k (1 - \lambda t/m)^m/(1 - \lambda t/m)^k. \quad (2.4.2)$$

As $h \to 0$, or equivalently as $m \to \infty$ (since $h = t/m$), the approximation (2.4.1) becomes exact and tends to the limit

$$[1/k!] (\lambda t)^k \exp(-\lambda t),$$

which can be seen by considering the limit of each individual term in (2.4.2), and using the fact that $(1 - x/m)^m \to \exp(-x)$ as $m \to \infty$; i.e. we have

$$\Pr[N = k] = (\lambda t)^k \exp(-\lambda t)/k! \qquad k = 0, 1, 2, \ldots .$$

This limiting discrete distribution is called the Poisson distribution; the underlying completely random series of point events from which it arises is often called the *Poisson process*. Its mean and variance are best computed by invoking the additivity of these quantities prior to taking the limit $h \to 0$. From Example 2.3, we have approximately

$$\bar{N} = mp \simeq m\lambda h = \lambda t,$$

$$\text{Var}(N) = mpq \simeq m\lambda h(1 - \lambda h) = \lambda t(1 - \lambda h),$$

which in the limit as $h \to 0$ becomes exact; i.e.

$$\bar{N} = \lambda t,$$
$$\mathrm{Var}(N) = \lambda t.$$

Its coefficient of variation is therefore $1/\surd(\lambda t)$, which means that the relative variation tends to diminish for long intervals.

2.4.2 The Interval Description

Next, we turn our attention to the interval description T, which specifies the length of the time interval between successive points. We shall first extract the key properties from the m discrete subintervals and then we shall take the limit to arrive at the exact continuous description. Supposing there is an arrival at the origin 0, then the probability that there is no arrival in the interval $(0, t)$ is $\Pr[T > t = mh]$, which is given by

$$\Pr[T > t = mh] = q^m \simeq (1 - .\lambda t/m)^m.$$

As $m \to \infty$, this tends to $\exp(-\lambda t)$, and we obtain the exact cumulative distribution function $F(t)$ of T; i.e. for $t \geq 0$

$$F(t) = \Pr[T \leq t] = 1 - \Pr[T > t] = 1 - \exp(-\lambda t).$$

The corresponding probability density function $f(t)$ is therefore, for $t \geq 0$,

$$f(t) = F'(t) = \lambda \exp(-\lambda t),$$

which is called the exponential distribution; this distribution is sketched in Fig. 2.6. From the above arguments, it is evident that the exponential distribution is merely a continuous form of the geometric distribution obtained by limiting operations. Again, its mean and variance are best computed prior to taking the limit $h \to 0$. Thus, from Example 2.2, the mean and variance of the trial number associated with the first success are approximately

Mean number of trials to 1st success $= 1/p \simeq 1/(\lambda h)$,

Var(number of trials to 1st success) $= q/p^2 \simeq (1 - \lambda h)/(\lambda h)^2$.

Since each trial corresponds to a time of h units, from (2.2.2) and (2.2.4) the above when converted to continuous time units become

Mean time to 1st arrival

$$\simeq h \times \text{mean number of trials to 1st success} = 1/\lambda,$$

Variance of time to 1st arrival

$$\simeq h^2 \times \text{Var(number of trials to 1st success)} = (1 - \lambda h)/\lambda^2.$$

In the limit as $h \to 0$, we obtain the exact mean and variance of the mean inter-point time interval

$$\bar{T} = 1/\lambda,$$

$$\mathrm{Var}(T) = 1/\lambda^2.$$

The corresponding coefficient of variation is thus 1. This value makes the exponential distribution a convenient yardstick for calibrating the randomness of other distributions; distributions will be referred to as more regular or less regular according as whether their coefficient of variation is <1 or >1

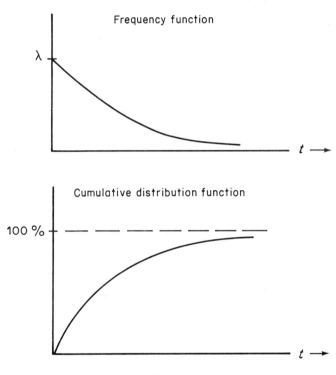

FIGURE 2.6.   The exponential distribution

In the above derivation, although we assumed that there was an arrival at the origin, we never actually made use of this fact. In fact, since the events that happen at different subintervals are independent, whether an arrival did take place at the origin really makes no difference, so that the distribution of the inter-arrival time is identical to the distribution of the time to the next arrival measured from an arbitrary time point. As what happened before the interval $(0, t)$ has no bearing on what happens in that interval, the exponential distribution is said to possess the *memoryless* property.

Example 2.4 Jobs arrive for processing at a computer centre following a Poisson stream. It is known that in a period of given length t, the probability that there is no arrival is 70%. Determine the mean and variance of the number of job arrivals in a time period of length $2t$.

Solution. Let T be the inter-arrival time of jobs, and $F(x)$ its cumulative distribution function. We are given that

$$\Pr[T > t] = 1 - F(t) = \exp(-\lambda t) = 0.7,$$

which implies

$$\lambda t = -\ln(0.7) = 0.36.$$

From Section 2.4.1, this is equal to both the mean and the variance of the number of job arrivals in a period of length t. The corresponding quantities for a period of length $2t$ is simply twice the above, and both are equal to 0.72. □

Example 2.5 Consider the occurrence of errors in the execution of a complex piece of software, where an error is regarded to be any (hardware or software) event which causes incorrect results to be produced. Suppose the occurrence of errors is completely random and that the probability that there is one or more errors in a 15-minute interval is given to be 5%. What is the error rate? If the total execution time is 3 hours, what is the probability that the entire execution is error-free?

Solution. Let λ be the error rate, T be the inter-error time, and $F(x)$ be the cumulative distribution function of T. We are given that

$$F(t) = 1 - \exp(-15\lambda) = 0.05,$$

which gives an error rate of

$$\lambda = [-\ln(0.95)]/15.$$

The required probability is

$$\Pr[T > 180] = \exp(-180\lambda) = 54\%. \quad \square$$

2.4.3 *Operations on Poisson Streams: Merging and Splitting*

In this section, we shall consider two common operations on Poisson event streams: the merging of several independent streams and the splitting of a single stream into several substreams.

We first consider the merging of two independent Poisson arrival streams with rates λ_1 and λ_2. Because of the nature of the Poisson process, the resulting merged stream will also be completely random in that the events at non-overlapping time intervals are independent. Now, in an arbitrary time interval of length t, the mean total number of points there coming from either stream is, by the additivity of the mean, $(\lambda_1 + \lambda_2)t$; thus the mean arrival rate of the merged stream is $(\lambda_1 + \lambda_2)$. In other words, the stream obtained from merging two independent Poisson streams is also a Poisson stream with rate equal to the sum of the constituent rates. This argument can be easily extended to the merging of an arbitrary number of independent Poisson streams as follows. The first two streams could be merged to form a new Poisson stream; this new stream could then be merged with the third to form a new Poisson one with rate equal to the sum of the rates of the first three streams. This process can be repeated until only a single stream remains. This final stream will be Poisson with rate equal to the sum of the rates of the component streams.

Next, we consider the splitting of a single Poisson stream of rate λ into n substreams in the following manner: each arrival is independently routed to the kth branch with probability p_k $(1 \leqslant k \leqslant n)$, with $\Sigma p_k = 1$. Let us focus our attention on the kth substream. Because the underlying source event stream is completely random, so too is this substream. Furthermore, in a short time interval of length h, a point event will only occur there only if (1) there is a corresponding point occurrence in the source stream, and (2) that point is routed to this branch; this happens with probability $p_k \lambda h$. Hence we conclude that the random splitting of a Poisson stream into n branches will give rise to n Poisson substreams, with the arrival rate of each substream given by the product of the arrival rate of the source stream and the routing probability to that substream.

Example 2.6 Consider a multiprocessor system consisting of n processors where the arrival of jobs for processing conforms to a Poisson process with rate λ. Assuming the arrival stream is randomly routed to each processor with equal probability, determine the distribution of the inter-arrival time to each processor. What is the corresponding coefficient of variation?

Solution. The arrival stream to each processor, being a branch of the original stream obtained by random routing, is thus a Poisson stream with rate λ/n. It will therefore give rise to an exponentially distributed inter-arrival time with mean n/λ; being exponentially distributed, the associated coefficient of variation is necessarily unity. $\square$

Example 2.7 Consider a multiprocessor system consisting of n processors, where the arrival of jobs for processing conforms to a Poisson process with rate λ as in the previous example. Suppose arrivals are now routed to individual processor in a cyclic manner so that every kth arrival is routed to the kth processor. Determine the coefficient of variation of the inter-arrival time of jobs to individual processors. Are these arrivals more regular or less regular than those in the random routing case?

Solution. This situation is different from that of random routing because the routing of successive jobs are not independent: if the previous arrival is routed to the kth processor, then the current one will not be routed to it. Because of the cyclical routing mechanism, the inter-arrival time T of jobs to individual processors is the sum of n random quantities

$$T = T_1 + T_2 + \cdots + T_n,$$

where each T_k is exponentially distributed with mean $1/\lambda$. Hence by the additivity of the mean and variance, we have $\bar{T} = n/\lambda$ and $\text{Var}(T) = n/\lambda^2$, giving a coefficient of variation, $C(T)$, of $1/\sqrt{n}$. This value of $C(T)$ is less than that in the exponential case which is unity; this signifies a smaller degree of relative variation and so represents a more regular arrival pattern than that in the random routing case. In fact, the probability density $f(t)$ of T, which results from summing n exponential quantities, is for $t \geq 0$ given by

$$f(t) = \lambda(\lambda t)^{n-1} \exp(-\lambda t)/(n-1)!;$$

this is known as the Erlang distribution with parameters n and λ. ∇

Example 2.8   Consider a system consisting of a single processor which accepts job submissions from a remote site as well as locally. It is known that the submission rate of the remote job stream is 1 job per hour and that both streams are Poisson. Supposing it is found that the standard deviation of the inter-arrival time of jobs arriving at the processor is 15 minutes, determine the job submission rate of the local stream.

Solution.   Let the unknown job rate be r jobs/hour. Then the job rate resulting from merging the local and remote streams is $r + 1$. Hence the mean inter-arrival time of the merged stream is $1/(r + 1)$; furthermore, since both streams are Poisson, so is the merged stream. This means that the inter-arrival time relating to the merged stream is exponentially distributed with the values for the standard deviation and the mean coincide; they are both equal to $\frac{1}{4}$ hour in this case. Equating this to $1/(r + 1)$, we obtain $r = 3$ jobs/hour as the job rate of the local stream. $\square$

2.4.4   The Importance of the Poisson Process

The exponential and the Poisson distributions really provide two alternative descriptions of the same phenomenon, one which is generated by a series of completely random events: for a given arrival rate λ, the inter-event time is exponentially distributed with mean $1/\lambda$, while the number of events in a time interval of duration t has a Poisson distribution with mean λt. They are, respectively, limiting forms of the geometric and binomial distributions. The Poisson process is important in performance evaluation for four reasons:

(1)   it introduces substantial simplification to performance analysis because of the memoryless property, by virtue of which it is not necessary to keep a detailed record of what happened earlier;

(2) an arrival stream obtained by pooling a large number of arbitrary sub-streams, in general, may be approximated by a Poisson process (a proof of this can be found in Khintchine (1960)); and such a pooling operation closely resembles a wide variety of mechanisms which generate point events in computer systems such as the failure of a large number of components and the submission of jobs by a large population of inter-active users;

(3) it is one of the few distributions where the probability mass function of the point description and the probability density function of the interval description both admit a simple, explicit representation;

(4) its completely random character remains unaltered by merging and splitting operations—these operations being extremely common in queueing networks analysis.

2.5 Summary

In performance evaluation, statements concerning system behaviour often need to be made in probability terms. Detailed descriptions of uncertainty are provided by the frequency function or, equivalently, the cumulative distribution function, whose salient features may be summarized by the mean and the variance. The former provides an indication of the typical value of the quantity; the latter provides a measure of the dispersion of values about the mean. The coefficient of variation expresses the standard deviation as a proportion of the mean and provides a dimensionless, often more meaningful, measure of dispersion.

Point events, such as the arrival of a job to the system, form an important class of events in performance evaluation. They are of infinitesimal duration and are characterized by their positions in time. Point events may be specified by an interval description, which focuses attention on the continuous inter-point time interval, or by a point description which counts the discrete number of points occurring in a given time interval. For a completely random series of point events where the occurrence of points in different time intervals are independent, the point description yields the Poisson distribution, while the interval description yields the exponential distribution—these being limiting forms of the binomial and geometric distributions respectively; the exponential distribution, in particular, exhibits the memoryless property in that what happens in any given time interval is not affected by what goes on before that interval. Moreover, the completely random character of these events are not destroyed when several streams are merged into one or when a single stream is split into several substreams.

2.6 Exercises

1. *Sequential file processing.* Consider a file consisting of N items from which we wish to locate a particular one. Suppose each item sustains the same

level of access activity—i.e. each item stands equal chance of being the required one—and that the items are examined sequentially from the beginning of the file. Find the mean and variance of the number of probes (i.e. number of items examined) in order to locate the required item.

2. Consider the processing of a sequential file as in Exercise 1. Suppose there are four items A, B, C and D in the file which, respectively, sustain 10%, 20%, 30%, and 40% of the access activity. Calculate the mean and variance of the number of probes for the following two arrangements: (a) the items are arranged in ascending order of access activity, (b) the items are arranged in descending order of access activity. Which is the preferable arrangement?

3. A job J consists of three independent job steps S1, S2 and S3 which are executed serially. The mean duration of each of the three steps is the same and equals 10 seconds, but their variances are respectively 0, 1, and 3. Find the mean and coefficient of variation of the execution time of the entire job.

4. A truncated geometric distribution taking values in the finite set $\{1, 2, \ldots, N\}$ has probability mass function of the following form

$$p(k) = Cb^k \qquad k = 1, 2, \ldots, N.$$

Express C in terms of b, and find the mean of this distribution.

5. A file enquiry system makes use of four data files stored on four different disks. Each enquiry requires access to only a single file, and each file is selected with equal probability. Supposing one of the disks is inoperational, calculate the mean and variance of the number of enquiries which cannot be answered in a batch of 100 enquiries.

6. Show that the mean of a continuous nonnegative random quantity X with cumulative distribution function $F(x)$ can be written as

$$\bar{X} = \int_0^\infty [1 - F(x)]\,dx.$$

Verify that this formula indeed yields the correct answer for the exponential distribution.

7. *Seek time of the moving head disk.* In a moving head disk, the seek operation consists of positioning the read/write head at the required cylinder. In the IBM 3330 moving head disk, the seek time S (in ms) and the seek distance D (measured in cylinders) are (approximately) related by the linear function: $S = 10 + D/10$. Express the mean and variance of S in terms of those of D.

8. *Service time of the moving head disk.* The service time of the moving head disk may be divided into three parts: (a) the seek time, which is the time taken to position the read/write head at the correct cylinder, (b) the latency time, which is the time spent in waiting for the beginning of the required record to come under the read/write head, and (c) the actual time taken to read the record. Suppose the latency plus transfer time is described by the uniform distribution over the interval [2, 18] as in Example 2.1, and that the seek distance has for its mean and variance the values of 135 and 9000 respectively. Calculate the mean and variance of the disk service time of the IBM 3330 disk using the seek characteristics given in Exercise 7.

9. Consider a hash table with 10 address slots each of which can hold two items. Suppose the hashing algorithm is such that each address is chosen with equal probability, and that there are 10 items to be placed in the table. For a given slot, calculate its overflow probability, i.e. the probability that it has more than two items assigned to it.

10. *Error detection and correction.* Consider the transmission of binary digits over a noisy communications channel in which errors occur independently, and that each bit has 10% chance of being transmitted incorrectly. To combat error, the following encoding scheme is introduced: instead of transmitting a digit once, the same digit is transmitted three times in a triplet, and the receiver decodes (i.e. corrects if necessary) a triplet to a 1 or 0 according to whether there are more 1s or 0s in the triplet. Calculate the probability that (a) transmission errors are present, (b) when errors are present, correction yields the right value, (c) when errors are present, correction yields the wrong value.

11. Suppose it is known that the duration of a terminal session is exponentially distributed with a mean of 30 minutes. Calculate the probability that the duration of a session is (a) less than 15 minutes, (b) more than one hour.

12. Suppose the failure of components in a computer system conforms to the Poisson process. In a given time period $(0, t)$, what is the probability that there is no failure? How does this relate to the complementary distribution function of the time to the first failure?

13. A data communications system uses two communications lines to transmit messages coming from a Poisson source with average message rate equal to five messages/second. Suppose it adopts a strategy whereby messages are routed to each line alternately. Show that the resultant traffic feeding into a given line is more regular than the Poisson process. Write down the frequency function of the corresponding inter-arrival time.

14. A multiprocessing system accepts job submissions from a Poisson source with average rate equal to six jobs/second. Suppose 10% of the total traffic is randomly routed to a particular processor. Determine (a) the inter-arrival time of jobs entering the processor, and (b) the probability that there are more than two arrivals to the processor in a one-minute interval.

CHAPTER 3

Resource Contention: *Basic Parameters and Measures of Effectiveness*

3.1 Basic Structure of a Queueing System

Contention of resources is a common phenomenon in computer systems. A resource, for example, may be a disk, CPU, printer, communications line, or I/O channel. Contention is present when the resource is unable to give immediate attention to all the requests demanding service from it; consequently, delay may be experienced by some requests in obtaining service. Resource contention generally gives rise to queueing. The delays caused by contention is mostly random in character, and its quantification is of central importance to performance assessment. In order to analyze contention delays, we first need to have a more exact specification of a queueing situation. A queueing situation is governed by the following factors: (a) the request arrival characteristics; (b) the service requirement and departure characteristics; (c) the service capacity; and (d) the service scheduling rule. We shall discuss each of these factors in turn.

3.1.1 *The Request Arrival Characteristics*

The arrival of a request can be regarded as a point event occurring in time, the characteristics of which have been discussed in detail in the previous chapter. In this book, we shall mostly be interested in completely random arrivals; the pattern of such arrivals is fully determined by the average arrival rate λ and gives rise to an exponentially distributed inter-arrival time with mean $1/\lambda$. Normally we would regard the number of possible arrivals as potentially infinite, but there are situations where it may not be realistic to do so. Consequently, it may sometimes be necessary to impose a bound on the number of possible arrivals into the system so that requests are regarded as being drawn from a finite, rather than infinite, population. An example of a finite population situation is an interactive system having a finite number of user terminals where each user can submit only at most one job for processing. In such a situation, the number of requests enqueued to the processor would affect the subsequent rate of arrivals, and in the extreme case, if all users are already enqueued to the processor, then no further arrivals could take place.

In this book, unless indicated otherwise, we always assume that the arrivals are drawn from an infinite population.

The term *input* is often used to refer to the pattern of the arrival stream; for example, completely random arrivals is often referred to as Poisson input. In a queueing context, the terms job, task, and customer are frequently used synonymously with request.

3.1.2 *The Service Requirement and Departure Characteristics*

A request arriving at the resource will require service from it, the duration of which is, in general, random in character. The service time or requirement of requests may be represented by a random quantity X which signifies the variable amount of 'work' brought into the system by each request. From the standpoint of the resource, a request is merely a 'packet' of work during whose service the resource will be tied up for an amount of X time units. Normally, a request departs from the system only after it has completed its service; in some situations, however, if requests cannot receive service immediately on arrival, they are not permitted to wait for the resource to be freed due to, for example, the unavailability of waiting room or buffer. In such a situation, a request may leave without receiving any service; such a system is commonly referred to as a *loss system*. An example of a loss system is a dial-up exchange consisting of a fixed number of trunk lines in which a call is not allowed to wait when no trunk lines are available. Frequently, however, there is some waiting room available so that a limited number of requests are permitted to wait for service, but when the waiting room is full newly arrived requests are turned away. In practice, of course, the capacity of the waiting room is always finite, but it is often sufficiently large so that effectively it may be regarded as infinite. This is, of course, a mathematical convenience which considerably simplifies the analysis, but it does furnish an acceptable approximation to reality; in this book, unless specifically stated otherwise, we always assume the waiting room to be infinite. The term *nonloss system* is often used to refer to a system in which all arriving requests always receive full service before departure; unless otherwise stated, all systems treated in this book is assumed to be nonloss.

In performance evaluation, the terms processing time and execution time are sometimes used instead of service time, while the terms server, facility, device, and processor are often used synonymously with resource.

3.1.3 *The Service Capacity*

The service capacity of a queueing system is dependent on the number of individual servers constituting the entire service function. When there is a single server, then working full capacity, it can deliver a maximum of one second of service or work every passing second; i.e. its service capacity is 1 second/second. In general, when there are m servers, the service capacity is stepped up to m times with a maximum of m seconds of work delivered every second. This, however, does not necessarily mean that the actual speed of service is always m times faster, but rather under the most favourable conditions where maximum concurrency can be exploited, it is possible for the m servers to deliver m seconds of service per second of elapsed time. For example, if there are 2 jobs in a system with 5 servers, the actual amount of work delivered is 2 seconds/second, but if there are 6 jobs present, then all 5 jobs could be serviced in parallel, with the system delivering 5 seconds/second. Note that we have made no explicit reference to the actual working speed of individual servers; such a specification is actually built into the service requirement description: for a slow server the mean service time would be large, while for a fast server the mean service time would be small.

It is sometimes convenient to express the service capacity in terms of the number of jobs processed per unit time. This is called the *service rate* and is obtained by dividing the service capacity in seconds (or a suitable time unit) by the average service requirement $\bar{X}$ of a job; it is measured in units of jobs per second. For example, a single server system can clear a maximum of 1 second of work every second; equivalently, it can clear a maximum of $(1/\bar{X})$ jobs every second. Likewise, for an m-server system, the service rate is m times that of a single server system and equals $(m/\bar{X})$ jobs/second.

3.1.4   *The Scheduling Rule*

The scheduling rule, sometimes called the scheduling discipline, specifies how jobs are to be selected among the pool of jobs awaiting service when a server becomes free. This rule is often based on job attributes such as the time of arrival, the service requirement, or the priority class. The commonest rule is the first-in–first-out (FIFO) rule which services jobs in arrival sequence and is based entirely on the job arrival time; similarly, the rule which sequences jobs in reversed order of arrival is called the last-in–first-out (LIFO) rule. The FIFO rule, for example, is often employed in disk units, and the LIFO rule is employed in stack processing. Central processor queues, on the other hand, usually employ a priority rule in which jobs are divided into different classes, and those with a high priority would receive service before those with a low priority, irrespective of their arrival times. In some cases, a priority rule may allow the service of a high priority job to interrupt that of a low priority job; such a rule is also widely implemented in operating systems and is called a preemptive priority scheduling rule.

3.2   A Shorthand Notation for the Specification of a Queueing System

Due to the number of components making up a queueing system, it is useful to be able to tell, at a glance, the salient features of a queue by suitably encoding the characteristics of these components. In this book, the four main descriptors of a queueing system discussed above will be represented as A/

B/m:S; where A represents the inter-arrival distribution; B, the service distribution; m, the number of servers; and S, the scheduling rule. The first two descriptors A and B are distribution specifications: a general distribution is signified by the letter G; the exponential distribution—with its memoryless property—is signified by the letter M; in the case of a degenerate or deterministic (i.e. constant) inter-arrival time, it is signified by the letter D. The abbreviations for the different scheduling rules will be introduced as we go along; however, if it is omitted from the specification, the default rule is taken to be FIFO.

Example 3.1 Describe the queues M/M/2 and D/G/1:LIFO. What is the difference between the queue M/M/1 and the queue M/G/1?

Solution. The queue M/M/2 signifies a two-server system with exponential inter-arrival time and exponential service time (usually with different mean values); since its service selection rule is omitted, it therefore selects jobs for service according to the default rule FIFO. The queue D/G/1:LIFO signifies a single server system with constant inter-arrival time and general service distribution; its service selection is based on the job arrival time, with the job having the largest arrival time being selected for service first. The queue M/M/1 is a special case of the queue M/G/1 because G signifies a general service distribution of arbitrary form, while M constrains the service distribution to the exponential form. Likewise, the queue M/D/1 is also an M/G/1 queue; here the service time is constrained to be a constant. When we represent a system as M/M/1 rather than M/G/1, we are really giving a more concrete specification of the system. □

Note that although our notation allows the salient characteristics of a queue to be encoded, it does not give a complete specification of the system because information concerning, for example, the arrival and service rates are not included. Thus, a given specification using the above notation really describes a family of queues with different (unspecified) parameters rather than uniquely pinpointing a single queue.

3.3 Work, Traffic Intensity, Utilization, and Throughput

As we have indicated above, the amount of work done by a queueing system is often measured in units of time: the arrival of each job brings into the system an average quantity of work equal to its mean service time $\bar{X}$. If there is an average number of λ job arrivals per second (or a suitable time unit), then the total amount of work presented to the system per second on average is $\lambda\bar{X}$ seconds; this is called the *traffic intensity*. In order for a system to cope adequately with this given level of demand, its service capacity should be greater than the demand; a system satisfying this condition is said to be *stable*.

For an m-server system, a maximum of m seconds of work can be completed every second so that this condition of stability can be written as

$$m > \lambda \bar{X}.$$

Note that we use strict inequality rather than $m \geqslant \lambda \bar{X}$ because in the case of equality there is no guarantee that the resultant system is able to cope adequately with the workload (see Example 3.2), and we wish to exclude such systems from the class of stable systems; in this book, we shall primarily be concerned with the performance of stable systems. A system satisfying the equality

$$m = \lambda \bar{X}$$

is said to be *saturated*; a saturated system is, by definition, unstable because it violates the stability condition $m > \lambda \bar{X}$. The saturation condition signifies that a system is working at its limits beyond which demand will certainly exceed the system capacity.

Example 3.2 Consider the queue $D/D/1$:LIFO with the arrival and service rates both equal to 1 second; i.e. we have $m = 1$, $\lambda = 1$, and $\bar{X} = 1$. The stability condition $m > \lambda \bar{X}$ is violated and the system is saturated. Suppose there is an initial backlog of two jobs when the system commences operation, then we note that the system is unable to cope adequately in the sense that (1) the system can never have any idle period because there is always work outstanding, and (2) some jobs will never be able to obtain service. □

If we denote the service rate $1/\bar{X}$ by μ, then the stability condition can also be written as $\lambda/\mu < m$. For a single server system, this is $\lambda < \mu$; this says that the service rate must exceed the arrival rate in order for the system to adequately cope, which is, of course, what one would expect intuitively. Since the average amount of work entering the system is λ/μ, then for an m-server system, the average amount of work presented per second to each server is $\lambda/(m\mu)$. Furthermore, since the service capacity of each server is 1 second/ second, this also represents the fraction of time that a server is engaged in doing work. That is, for an m-server system, the server *utilization* ρ is given by

$$\rho = \lambda/(m\mu).$$

For a single server system, the fraction of time that the server is busy is therefore $\rho = \lambda/\mu$, which we note is the same as the traffic intensity. Intuitively, one would expect the server utilization equal to the long-run probability of finding the server busy, and this is indeed the case for a general single server queue; a demonstration of this fact may be found in Kleinrock (1975). Thus for a single server system, $1 - \lambda/\mu$ can be regarded as the probability of finding the server idle, and the stability condition $\lambda/\mu < 1$ merely ensures that there is a positive probability that the server is idle. Consequently, for a single server queue, describing it as stable and describing it as one in which the server occasionally becomes idle are entirely equivalent descriptions, since both correspond to the same condition $\lambda/\mu < 1$. The *throughput* of a system refers to the average number of requests serviced by the system per unit time; for a nonloss stable system, it would have no difficulty in coping with all the demands and its throughput is simply the input rate λ. The maximum throughput of a system is related to the limiting number of job arrivals that the system could support, and is defined as the arrival rate which gives rise to system saturation; for a given service rate μ, the maximum throughput for an m-server system is therefore $m\mu$.

Example 3.3 In a computer network, messages having an average length of 500 bits are being transmitted across a communications line at an average rate of 20/second. (a) Determine the minimum line speed required to handle this traffic. (b) Supposing it is required to keep the line utilization below 80%, calculate the minimum line speed required to achieve this. (c) What is the resultant maximum throughput if the minimum line speed of (b) is used?

Solution. Let v be the line speed in bps (bits per second). Then the time taken to transmit 500 bits is $500/v$ seconds. The line utilization is therefore $20 \times 500/v$ which must be less than 1 for a stable system. This implies that, in order to have a stable system, we must have $20 \times 500/v < 1$ or $v > 10\,000$ bps. The minimum line speed must be greater than 10 000 bps. If the line utilization must be kept below 80%, then we must have $20 \times 500/v < 0.8$ or $v > 12\,500$ bps. If $v = 12\,500$, then the maximum throughput Λ must satisfy $500\Lambda/12\,500 = 1$; this implies that the maximum throughput is $\Lambda = 25$ messages/second. $\square$

Example 3.4 Consider a multi-processing system in which jobs requiring an average processing time of 100 ms are arriving at the rate of 60/second. (a) Calculate the minimum number of processors required to cope with this demand. (b) If the minimum number of processors in (a) is used, what are the resultant maximum throughput and processor utilization?

Solution. Let m be the number of processors. The traffic intensity is $\lambda\bar{X} = 0.1 \times 60 = 6$. In order to have a stable system, we must have $m > \lambda\bar{X}$ so that the minimum number of processors is $m = 7$. The resultant processor utilization is $\lambda\bar{X}/m = 6/7 = 85.7\%$. The maximum throughput Λ must satisfy the saturation condition $m = \Lambda\bar{X}$; this implies $\Lambda = 7/0.1 = 70$ jobs/second. $\square$

3.4 Measures of Effectiveness

Measures of effectiveness may be broadly divided into two related categories depending on whether the situation is viewed from the users' or the system's standpoint.

3.4.1 *User-oriented Measures*

From the user's standpoint, performance is often judged in terms of how quickly the results are returned from processing. A user is interested in the elapsed time between the moment of job submission and the moment the results are delivered; this elapsed time is often referred to as the *response time* in the case of interactive systems, and as the *turnaround time* in the case of batch systems. Evidently, a system with a low value for this elapsed time is to be preferred. In this book, the term response time rather than turnaround time will be used to refer to this elapsed time. The mean response time can be broken down into two components: the mean service time and the mean waiting time. The *waiting time* is defined to be the non-service component of the response time; in most cases, when there is no interruption to the service of a job once it commences, the waiting time is simply the elapsed time between job submission and service commencement. If $\bar{R}$ denotes the mean response time, $\bar{X}$ denotes the mean service time, and $\bar{W}$ denotes the mean waiting time, then we have

$$\bar{R} = \bar{X} + \bar{W}.$$

Being part of the specification, the variability of the service time is, of course, given so that once the waiting time is known the response time could be determined. Unlike the service time—which is governed by a single job—the waiting time is governed by the interaction of a stream of jobs with the system, and is dependent on factors such as the number of jobs enqueued, the server utilization, and the scheduling rule.

3.4.2 *System-oriented Measures*

While users primarily focus attention on the progress of individual jobs through the system, the system itself is more concerned with collective behaviour and adopts a global view of the situation. The system is more interested in factors such as utilization, throughput, the number of requests in the system, and the length of the busy period. A high utilization and throughput indicate that a resource is effectively and economically exploited with very little wasted capacity. The number of jobs in the system—which consists of those in service as well as those awaiting service—obviously affects the buffer allocation and management policies. The length of the busy period measures the amount of time that the system has to work continuously commencing from the moment of a job arriving to an empty system and terminating at the moment when the system next becomes empty following the departure of a job. As the busy period expands, the amount of slack in the system is eroded and results, in general, in increased utilization.

Whether a system performs satisfactorily or not is, to a large extent, dependent on whether it is viewed from the users' standpoint or the system's standpoint, and the interests represented by these two standpoints are very different. For example, the users typically like to see a relatively under-utilized system so that when they need to use it, the chance of queueing is small; in this way, their response time is unlikely to be excessive. On the other hand, from the system's standpoint, an under-utilized system signifies uneconomic usage; it represents an unsatisfactory situation and possibly indicates inefficient deployment of system resources. In the next chapter, we shall look at relationships which explicitly link the resource utilization to the user response time.

3.5 Summary

Resource contention gives rise to congestion and queueing. A queueing situation may be specified by (1) the arrival characteristics, (2) the service characteristics, (3) the service capacity, and (4) the scheduling rule. This information may be conveniently represented as A/B/m:S; where A and B signify respectively the inter-arrival and service distributions; m the number of servers; and S the scheduling rule.

The traffic intensity measures the total service demand on the system per unit time and equals the product of the average request arrival rate and the mean request service requirement; for an m-server system, the server utilization is the traffic intensity divided by m. A stable system is one in which the service capacity exceeds the traffic intensity; a stable system can always cope adequately with the work demanded of it. For a stable nonloss system, the request input rate is sometimes referred to as the system throughput. The response time of a job refers to the elapsed time between its submission and the return of the results; it is made up of a service time component and a waiting time component. Typical measures of system performance are: response time, waiting time, queue size, throughput, and utilization. The first two are of particular interest to the individual users while the remaining three are of particular interest to those who manage the system operation.

3.6 Exercises

1. Consider a two-server system which services requests in order of arrival. It is found that the coefficient of variation of the inter-arrival time is zero, and that the mean and standard deviation of the service time coincide. Characterize this system using the notation of Section 3.2.

2. Similar tasks arrive for processing at a given processor at the rate of 0.1 task per microsecond. Suppose the processor operates at a speed of 0.75 mips

(million instructions per second). Derive a bound on the average number of instructions in a task if the system is to operate in a stable manner.

3. Two types of messages are transmitted over 12 communications lines. Most of the messages are short ones with a mean duration of 10 ms but occasionally there are long messages requiring a mean transmission duration of 1 second. If the message arrival rate is 80/second, and that the proportion of short messages is 90%, determine (i) the traffic intensity, and (ii) the line utilization.

4. An m-processor system is observed to have a utilization of 90%. The mean service time of jobs is 5 ms. Determine the reduction in server utilization if the number of processors is increased by 2.

5. A four-server queue is found to have a server utilization of 60%. Calculate the average amount of work entering the system in (a) a 10-minute interval, and (b) a 60-minute interval.

6. A communications line has a utilization of 70%. Calculate the change in utilization if the arrival rate is increased by 10% and the mean service time is decreased by 8%.

7. The server utilization of a five-server queue is known to be 85%. What will be the resultant utilization if the same traffic is fed into a three-server system in which the servers work twice as fast?

CHAPTER 4

Fundamental Relationships and their Applications

4.1 Relationships Between Delay and Queue Size: Little's Formulae

Intuitively, one would expect that the response time and the number of jobs in the system are closely related because if an arrival should find a large number of jobs present, then a long wait for service seems likely. In fact, the connection between these two quantities is expressible as a simple proportionality relationship linking the corresponding mean values: if $\bar{J}$ denotes the mean number of jobs in the system, and $\bar{R}$ the mean response time, then we have

$$\bar{J} = \lambda \bar{R}, \tag{4.1.1}$$

where the constant of proportionality λ is simply the average job arrival rate. To some extent, this relationship is intuitively evident in the case of a single server system operating the FIFO rule. Consider a typical job arrival. On average, it spends $\bar{R}$ units of time in the system before departure, and on its departure it notes down the mean number of jobs $\bar{J}$ in the system. Under FIFO scheduling, these job arrivals can take place only while the job in question is progressing through the system. Since the average job arrival rate is λ, the average number of arrivals $\bar{J}$ during this period of average duration $\bar{R}$ is accordingly $\lambda \bar{R}$. Under this interpretation, the relation (4.1.1) merely says that the number of jobs left behind in the system as observed by a departing job may be regarded as a representative sample of system behaviour. A corresponding relationship also holds between the mean queue length $\bar{Q}$ (excluding the one in service) and the mean waiting time $\bar{W}$ (excluding the service time):

$$\bar{Q} = \lambda \bar{W}. \tag{4.1.2}$$

A similar intuitive justification of this also applies in the case of FIFO scheduling: the average number of jobs arrived during the waiting time of a typical job is simply the average arrival rate times the average waiting time.

The relationships (4.1.1) and (4.1.2) are often referred to as Little's formulae; they were first proved in Little (1961) under rather general conditions. These conditions are generally met by systems considered in this book, so Little's formulae may be applied without fear of error. Although we have provided intuitive justification of them only in the special case of the FIFO rule, these mean value relationships are in fact valid under quite general settings irrespective of the scheduling rule, the arrival and service characteristics, and the number of servers. A detailed discussion of the conditions under which Little's formulae hold may be found in Jewell (1967). Since the response time can be decomposed into the service and waiting times,

$$\bar{R} = \bar{X} + \bar{W}, \qquad (4.1.3)$$

there also exists, on multiplication by the average arrival rate and applying Little's formulae, a corresponding decomposition of the number of jobs in the system:

$$\bar{J} = \lambda\bar{X} + \bar{Q}. \qquad (4.1.4)$$

This means that knowledge of any one of the four quantities $\bar{R}, \bar{W}, \bar{J}, \bar{Q}$ allows the remaining three to be determined in a straightforward manner, provided the mean service time and the arrival rate are known. For example, knowing $\bar{Q}$ allows $\bar{J}$ and $\bar{W}$ to be respectively obtained from (4.1.4) and (4.1.2), and from (4.1.3), $\bar{R}$ could then be obtained.

Example 4.1 For a $G/G/1$ queue, suppose it is given that the mean arrival and service rates are respectively 3 and 5 jobs/second. Supposing it is found that the mean queue length is $\bar{Q} = 6.7$, determine the mean number of jobs in the system and the mean response time.

Solution. Here $\lambda = 3$ and $\mu = 5$ so that the traffic intensity is 0.6. From (4.1.4), the mean number of jobs in the system is $\bar{J} = 0.6 + 6.7 = 7.3$. From (4.1.1), the mean response time $\bar{R} = 7.3/3 = 2.4$ seconds. □

The next question is: how do we determine any of them in the first place?

4.2 The Mean Response Time

In this section, we shall concentrate on the single server queue with Poisson input and general service pattern operating the FIFO rule, i.e. the queue $M/G/1$. As in the previous section, the rate of job arrival will be denoted by λ. In Section 4.2.1, we consider a situation where the service requirements of all the jobs are identical. In Section 4.2.2, we consider a useful generalization in which the service requirement of jobs initiating the facility from idle is allowed to be different; this will allow us to cater for situations where there is a set-up overhead or a warm-up delay.

4.2.1 *The Pollaczek–Khintchine Formulae*

We shall first focus our attention on the mean waiting time $\bar{W}$ and present an intuitive derivation of it. Consider a typical job arriving into the system. Its waiting time would consist of (1) the complete service times of all the jobs already in the queue, which on average equals $\bar{Q}\bar{X}$, plus (2) the residual service time of any job whose service is in progress; i.e.

$$\bar{W} = \bar{Q}\bar{X} + \bar{S},$$

where $\bar{S}$ is the mean residual service time. Since from (4.1.2), $\bar{Q} = \lambda\bar{W}$, carrying out this substitution and solving for $\bar{W}$, we have

$$\bar{W} = \bar{S}/(1 - \lambda\bar{X}). \tag{4.2.1}$$

It is shown in Appendix 4A that

$$\bar{S} = \tfrac{1}{2}\lambda\overline{X^2}, \tag{4.2.2}$$

from which we immediately obtain, on denoting $\lambda\bar{X}$ by ρ, the key result in queueing theory:

$$\bar{W} = \lambda\overline{X^2}/[2(1 - \rho)]. \tag{4.2.3}$$

This is often called the *Pollaczek–Khintchine formula*. (A more rigorous demonstration of it may be found, for example, in Kleinrock (1975).) If we make use of the coefficient of variation of the service time $C(X)$, this can also be written as

$$\bar{W} = \rho\bar{X}[1 + C(X)^2]/[2(1 - \rho)]. \tag{4.2.4}$$

It is frequently convenient to express the mean waiting time as a proportion of the mean service time; this is a dimensionless quantity called the *normalized mean waiting time* and is denoted by the symbol $\bar{W}^*$:

$$\bar{W}^* = \bar{W}/\bar{X} = \rho[1 + C(X)^2]/[2(1 - \rho)]. \tag{4.2.5}$$

From this, we see that for a given $C(X)$, we have in general

$$\bar{W}^* \propto \rho/(1 - \rho), \tag{4.2.6}$$

and the proportionality becomes equality in the special case of the exponential service distribution where $C(X) = 1$. The normalized mean waiting time as a function of ρ for this case is sketched in Fig. 4.1. Because of the general proportionality relationship (4.2.6), the normalized mean waiting time for other service distribution would admit somewhat similar characteristics to this case: $\bar{W}^*$ initially rises rather gently but the increase becomes progressively steeper, and diverges to ∞ as $\rho \to 1$. As indicated in the previous section, one can obtain from (4.2.4) the mean response time $\bar{R}$, the mean number of

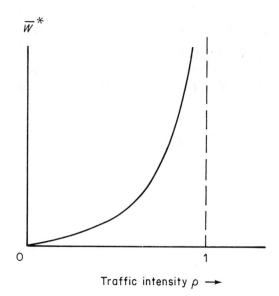

$$\overline{W}^*$$

O   1

Traffic intensity $\rho \longrightarrow$

FIGURE 4.1. The M/M/1 normalized mean waiting time

jobs in the system $\bar{J}$, and the mean queue length $\bar{Q}$ in a straightforward manner by Little's formula. That is

$$\bar{R} = \rho \bar{X}[1 + C(X)^2]/[2(1 - \rho)] + \bar{X}, \tag{4.2.7}$$

$$\bar{J} = \rho^2[1 + C(X)^2]/[2(1 - \rho)] + \rho, \tag{4.2.8}$$

$$\bar{Q} = \rho^2[1 + C(X)^2]/[2(1 - \rho)]. \tag{4.2.9}$$

All these equations really represent different aspects of the same basic result, and are frequently referred to as the Pollaczek–Khintchine formulae. In this book, the term Pollaczek–Khintchine formula will be used to signify any formula which expresses $\bar{R}$, $\bar{W}$, $\bar{J}$, or $\bar{Q}$ in terms of the basic input and service characteristics of the M/G/1 queue.

Example 4.2 A communications line receives input messages from two independent sources; each source follows a Poisson stream with rate equal to 1 message/minute. Suppose messages are transmitted in order of arrival and that the mean and standard deviation of the message transmission time are 20 seconds and 5 seconds respectively. Calculate the mean message response time and the mean number of messages in the queue.

Solution. Since the result of merging two independent Poisson streams is also a Poisson stream with rate equal to the sum of the two rates, the input to this line is therefore Poisson with rate equals 2 messages/minute. The situation can be represented by an M/G/1 queue and so we can use the

Pollaczek–Khintchine formula. In order to calculate the mean response time $\bar{R}$, we have to first calculate the line utilization and the coefficient of variation of the transmission time. Here $\lambda = 2$ and $\mu = 3$ so that the utilization $\rho = \frac{2}{3}$. The coefficient of variation of the transmission time is $C(X) = \frac{5}{20} = \frac{1}{4}$. Substituting these values into (4.2.7), we obtain

$$\bar{R} = (\tfrac{2}{3})(\tfrac{1}{3})(1 + \tfrac{1}{16})/[2(1 - \tfrac{2}{3})] + \tfrac{1}{3} = 0.69 \text{ minutes or } 41.3 \text{ seconds.}$$

The mean number of jobs in the queue from (4.2.9) is

$$\bar{Q} = (\tfrac{2}{3})^2(1 + \tfrac{1}{16})/[2(1 - \tfrac{2}{3})] = 0.71. \quad \square$$

Example 4.3 (Bulk arrival) Consider a processing system in which jobs are grouped into batches before submission. Suppose the batch size is constant and equals b, and that the batch arrival stream is Poisson with rate λ'. Suppose the mean and variance of the individual job service time are $\bar{X}$ and V respectively. Determine the mean response time of an individual job, assuming each job can be placed equally likely in any one of the b positions within a batch. What is the effect of batching on performance and what is the optimal batch size?

Solution. Viewing a batch as a single request, the mean batch waiting time B (excluding service) can be obtained from the Pollaczek–Khintchine formula. The mean and variance of the batch service time are, by additivity, $b\bar{X}$ and bV respectively. Thus we have

$$B = \lambda'(b\bar{X})^2[1 + bV/(b\bar{X})^2]/[2(1 - \lambda'b\bar{X})].$$

Since there are b jobs to a batch, $\lambda = \lambda'b$ may be regarded as the job arrival rate. Denoting the utilization $\lambda'b\bar{X} = \lambda\bar{X}$ by ρ, the above may be written as

$$B = \lambda(b\bar{X}^2 + V)/[2(1 - \rho)].$$

Since a job can be placed anywhere within a batch with the same probability $1/b$, the average remaining delay once a batch commences service is $\bar{X}(1 + 2 + \cdots + b)/b = \bar{X}(b + 1)/2$; this means that the total job response time $\bar{R}$ is $B + \bar{X}(b + 1)/2$; i.e.

$$\bar{R} = \lambda(b\bar{X}^2 + V)/[2(1 - \rho)] + \bar{X}(b + 1)/2.$$

We notice that $\bar{R}$ increases as b increases which means that batching has a harmful effect on response time. This is in fact not surprising because there is an element of built-in congestion here: all jobs in a batch arrive at the same time and all except possibly the first one must be delayed (the first one can commence service immediately only if the system is idle). We also note from the above expression that the minimum value for $\bar{R}$ is when $b = 1$; in this case, the system reduces to the normal M/G/1 queue with the built-in congestion removed. $\square$

4.2.2   The Generalized Pollaczek–Khintchine Formulae

In the previous section, we dealt with service times which were identical; here we consider a simple generalization in which jobs initiating the facility from idle—which are called *initiators*—are allowed to have a service time distribution different from that of other jobs. In this context, the term non-initiators will be used to refer to jobs which are not initiators. This generalization is extremely useful for analysing disk storage units and database performance, and for analyzing facilities which require additional set-up time or warm-up period when starting from 'cold'; indeed, some of the key results of Chapter 9 are directly obtainable using this generalization. If Y denotes the service time of initiators and X that of non-initiators, then (4.2.1) is also applicable to this situation except that the average residual service time must be replaced by a different value. It is shown in Appendix 4B that the mean residual service time $\bar{S}$ in this case is given by

$$\bar{S} = \tfrac{1}{2}\lambda[\rho\overline{X^2} + (1 - \rho)\overline{Y^2}]$$

where ρ is the utilization factor, and in the present situation it is given by

$$\rho = \lambda\bar{Y}/[1 - \lambda(\bar{X} - \bar{Y})], \qquad (4.2.10)$$

so that the mean waiting time $\bar{W}$ becomes

$$\bar{W} = \tfrac{1}{2}\lambda[\rho\overline{X^2} + (1 - \rho)\overline{Y^2}]/(1 - \lambda\bar{X}). \qquad (4.2.11)$$

We note that (4.2.11) immediately reduces to (4.2.4) when $Y = X$. (A more rigorous derivation of (4.2.11) may be found, for example, in Leung and Choo (1982).) Since the mean service time is $\bar{Y}$ if the system is found to be empty on arrival—this occurs with probability $(1 - \rho)$—and is $\bar{X}$ otherwise, the mean service time here is

$$\bar{Z} = \rho\bar{X} + (1 - \rho)\bar{Y} = \bar{Y}/[1 - \lambda(\bar{X} - \bar{Y})], \qquad (4.2.12)$$

so that the normalized mean waiting time is

$$\bar{W}^* = \bar{W}/\bar{Z} = \tfrac{1}{2}\lambda[\lambda\bar{Y}\,\overline{X^2} + (1 - \lambda\bar{X})\,\overline{Y^2}]/[\bar{Y}(1 - \lambda\bar{X})].$$

The mean response time $\bar{R} = \bar{W} + \bar{Z}$ can be obtained by adding (4.2.11) and (4.2.12). The mean number of jobs $\bar{J}$ in the system and the mean queue length $\bar{Q}$ can be obtained by application of Little's formulae; i.e. $\bar{J} = \lambda\bar{R}$ and $\bar{Q} = \lambda\bar{W}$. These formulae, which express $\bar{R}$, $\bar{W}$, $\bar{J}$ or $\bar{Q}$ in terms of the basic input and service characteristics, will be referred to in this book as the *generalized Pollaczek–Khintchine formulae*; they are more general than the ordinary Pollaczek–Khintchine formulae and automatically reduce to them in the special case when $Y = X$. The condition for a stable system here is $\lambda\bar{Z} < 1$. From (4.2.12), this implies $\lambda\bar{X} < 1$; this is intuitively reasonable because if the system utilization is high, the effect of initiators is negligible, so that only the service requirement of non-initiators enters into consideration in determining stability.

Example 4.4 (Fixed Head Disk Processing). Consider the processing of records on a fixed head disk unit in which the time required for one revolution is 10 ms. If the size of a record is a complete track (i.e. full track blocking), then the service time of non-initiators is 10 ms, since the reading of a record commences and terminates at the same point—the index marker—on a track. For initiators, however, an additional rotational delay is incurred. Suppose the request arrival is Poisson with rate equal to 10/second, and that the mean and variance of the additional rotational delay for initiators are 5 and 8.3 respectively. Determine the mean request response time. What is the error if no distinction is made between initiators and non-initiators?

Solution. Since the service time for initiators is constant, its variance is zero; its mean and second moment are

$$\bar{X} = 10;$$
$$\overline{X^2} = \mathrm{Var}(X) + (\bar{X})^2 = 100.$$

The mean service time for initiators is $\bar{Y} = 15$; its variance is, by additivity, $\mathrm{Var}(Y) = 8.3 + 0 = 8.3$. Thus

$$\overline{Y^2} = \mathrm{Var}(Y) + 15^2 = 233.3.$$

From (4.2.10), the utilization is

$$\rho = 0.01 \times 15/(1 + 0.01 \times 5) = 0.14 \text{ or } 14\%.$$

From (4.2.12), the overall mean service time is

$$\bar{Z} = 0.14 \times 10 + 0.86 \times 15 = 14.3 \text{ ms}.$$

From (4.2.11), the mean waiting time is

$$\bar{W} = 0.01(0.14 \times 100 + 0.86 \times 233.3)/[2(1 - 0.01 \times 10)] = 1.19 \text{ ms}.$$

Thus the mean response time is

$$\bar{R} = 1.19 + 14.3 = 15.49 \text{ ms}.$$

If the initial rotational delay of initiators is ignored, then from the Pollaczek–Khintchine formula, the mean request waiting time is

$$0.01 \times 100/[2(1 - 0.01 \times 10)] = 0.56 \text{ ms},$$

giving a mean response time of 10.56 ms. The error in the mean response time resulting from this simplification is

$$(15.49 - 10.56)/15.49 = 31.8\%.$$

In ignoring the initial rotational delay of initiators, the device utilization is $\lambda \bar{X} = 10\%$. Compared with the true utilization of 14% given above, this yields an error of 28.6%. □

Example 4.5 A letter quality printer operates at a printing speed of 2 pages/ minute. Suppose the arrival of print requests follows a Poisson stream at an average rate of 1 every 30 minutes and that the requirement of each job can range from 1 to 30 pages with all sizes (in number of integral pages) within this range equally likely. It is sometimes necessary to reset the printer when starting it from idle; if a reset is required, then it takes a constant time of 1 minute, and it is given that such reset is required 50% of the time. Determine the average waiting time of a print request.

Solution. We shall first determine the characteristics of the service time X for non-initiators. Since the print requirement of a request having a given size within the range 1 to 30 occurs with probability $\frac{1}{30}$, the mean number of pages per job is $(1 + 2 + \cdots + 30)/30 = 15.5$; the corresponding second moment is

$$(1^2 + 2^2 + \cdots + 30^2)/30 = (30 \times 31 \times 61)/(6 \times 30) = 315.16.$$

To convert these to time requirements in minutes, we multiply the mean by $\frac{1}{2}$ and the second moment by $(\frac{1}{2})^2$; thus we have

$$\bar{X} = 7.75$$
$$\overline{X^2} = 78.79,$$

so that its variance is $78.79 - 7.75^2 = 18.73$. The mean and variance of the reset time are

$$\text{Mean} = \tfrac{1}{2}(1 + 0) = 0.5$$
$$\text{Variance} = \tfrac{1}{2}[(1 - \tfrac{1}{2})^2 + (0 - \tfrac{1}{2})^2] = 0.25.$$

Thus the mean and variance of the service time Y for initiators are

$$\bar{Y} = 7.75 + 0.5 = 8.25$$
$$\text{Var}(Y) = 18.73 + 0.25 = 18.98,$$

which implies that

$$\overline{Y^2} = 18.98 + 8.25^2 = 87.04.$$

The printer utilization, from (4.2.10), is $\rho = (8.25/30)/(1 + 0.5/30) = 0.27$. Substituting the above values into (4.2.11), we obtain the mean waiting time $\bar{W} = 1.91$ minutes. $\square$

4.3 Classification of Arrival Characteristics

So far, we have been mainly concentrating on Poisson input which, as explained in Section 2.5, is equivalent to having an inter-arrival time T which is exponentially distributed. The exponential inter-arrival time is generated by completely random arrivals and is characterized by a coefficient of variation $C(T)$ of unity. In general, for the same average arrival rate, the performance of a system with completely random arrival is less desirable than that of a system with a constant inter-arrival time because in the former, arrivals are unevenly spaced—sometimes clustering close together—with the result that at certain times the server may have to deal with several arrivals within a short period, while at other times it may stand idle with no work to do. This necessarily exacerbates congestion. On the other hand, if the inter-arrival time is constant—the associated coefficient of variation $C(T)$ being zero—then workload is fed into the system at a steady rate with no sudden surge of demand on the system and so smooths out the effect of congestion. A value $C(T)$ lying between 0 and 1 exhibits arrival characteristics somewhere between those of constant arrival and completely random arrival. As a practical guideline, a value of $C(T)$ lying in the range 1 ± 0.15 may reasonably be approximated by Poisson input. A value of $C(T)$ falling below 0.85 tends to be relatively evenly spaced, while a value exceeding 1.15 tends to have arrivals clustered together. Hence the Poisson assumption tends to over-estimate congestion for cases with $C(T) < 1$ but under-estimate congestion for those with $C(T) > 1$, although in practice a value of $C(T) > 1$ should be relatively uncommon.

4.4 Classification of Service Characteristics

From the Pollaczek–Khintchine formula, it is evident that the coefficient of variation of the service time $C(X)$ is a key determinant of performance. It can be seen from (4.2.7) that for the same mean service time and server utilization, the mean response time is an increasing function of $C(X)$; accordingly, the M/G/1 queue which gives minimal delay is that with constant service time—i.e. the queue M/D/1—since in that case $C(X) = 0$. The normalized mean waiting time of the M/D/1 queue is

$$\bar{W}^* = \rho/[2(1 - \rho)].$$

The queue M/M/1 on the other hand has a normalized mean waiting time exactly doubled that of the above, since its coefficient of variation is 1, so that from the Pollaczek–Khintchine formula, we have

$$\bar{W}^* = \rho/(1 - \rho).$$

For most systems encountered in practice, the coefficient of variation of the service time normally lies between 0 and 1, so that the mean normalized waiting time $\bar{W}^*$ for these queues would lie between the bounds

$$\tfrac{1}{2}\rho/(1 - \rho) \leqslant \bar{W}^* \leqslant \rho/(1 - \rho). \tag{4.4.1}$$

The size of this range is $\tfrac{1}{2}\rho/(1 - \rho)$, which becomes more compressed as the traffic intensity ρ decreases. Accordingly, the bounds (4.4.1) are especially tight under light traffic conditions because the difference between the upper and lower bounds is small. This also suggests that the influence of the precise form of the service distribution is insignificant when the traffic is light. Similarly, in cases where $C(X) > 1$, which signifies a high degree of variation and unpredictability in the service time, the normalized mean waiting time will always exceed $\rho/(1 - \rho)$.

Example 4.6 Suppose it is observed that the normalized mean waiting time of requests for a particular I/O device is less than 2. Assuming the arrival stream is Poisson, determine an upper bound on the device utilization.

Solution. It is given that the normalized mean waiting time $\bar{W}^* < 2$; combining this with (4.4.1) we have

$$\tfrac{1}{2}\rho/(1 - \rho) \leq \bar{W}^* < 2.$$

Thus we have $4(1 - \rho) > \rho$, which implies that the device utilization is less than 80%. □

4.5 A Reliable Operating Environment: Conservative Systems

In the previous sections, attention has been primarily focused on the FIFO rule; proceeding from the FIFO assumption, we obtained the Pollaczek–Khintchine formulae for the M/G/1 queue. In fact, the Pollaczek–Khintchine formulae are also valid for other scheduling rules under certain conditions. These conditions are:

(1) the system in question is *conservative* (explained below);
(2) the selection criterion used by the scheduling rule is not based on the service time;
(3) the scheduling rule is non-preemptive.

A conservative system is one within which no work is created or destroyed. Work is, for example, created if the facility becomes inoperable when there is work outstanding, and work is destroyed if a job departs from the system (e.g. intentionally cancelled by the user or abnormally terminated due to errors) without either commencing service or attaining the full service; in such cases, the quantity of work that needs to be done cannot be determined from the arrival and service characteristics alone, but depends on how the workload is altered by other factors. Hence, a conservative system presupposes a certain degree of system reliability in which unexpected failure events are rare. In an unreliable operating environment, a server can break down in the presence of outstanding work—thereby creating work—or a job can be unexpectedly aborted due to (hardware or software) errors—thereby destroying work.

If the scheduling rule selects jobs for service according to their service requirements, then the Pollaczek–Khintchine formulae no longer applies. For example, in the case of selection based on shortest-job-first (SJF) where the facility gives priority treatment to short jobs, then the resulting delay will in general be different from that given by the Pollaczek–Khintchine formula. If a scheduling rule permits a job's service to be interrupted before completion, then it is called preemptive; such a rule, too, will invalidate the above invariance property and in general gives rise to an average response time different from that given by the Pollaczek–Khintchine formula. A system meeting the above three conditions will, for convenience, be denoted by M/G/1:CONS in this book; for such a system, the mean response time and related measures may be computed from the Pollaczek–Khintchine formula. It should be pointed out, however, that the invariance in the response time with respect to the scheduling rule applies to the mean value only and cannot be extended to the corresponding distribution or higher moments. In the case of the number of jobs in the system, on the other hand, the invariance property does extend to the corresponding distribution.

Example 4.7 (Stack Processing). Consider a stack in which the insertion of new items conforms to a Poisson process with rate equal to 8 items/ms. The scheduling rule here is LIFO. Supposing the time to dequeue an item is constant and equals 0.1 ms, determine the mean number of items in the stack.

Solution. This system is an instance of the M/G/1:CONS queue since the LIFO discipline is non-preemptive and does not select job according to their service requirement. This means that the mean number of items can be obtained from the Pollaczek–Khintchine formula. In this situation, we have $C(X) = 0$ and $\rho = 0.8$, and so the mean number of items $\bar{J}$ in the stack is $\bar{J} = \frac{1}{2} \times 0.8^2/(1 - 0.8) + 0.8 = 2.4$. ∇

In fact, the type of invariance in the mean response time and mean queue size described above also extends to queues with general input and certain priority systems. A detailed proof of this property may be found in Kleinrock (1976); its extension to priority systems will be considered in the next chapter.

4.6 Summary

Little's formulae (4.1.1) and (4.1.2) express general relationships between the number of jobs and the delay in a queueing system. By virtue of these formulae, knowledge of any one of the four quantities—mean response time, mean waiting time, mean number of jobs in the system, and mean queue size—would allow the remaining three to be obtained in a straightforward manner. In the case of a single server system with Poisson input, any one of these quantities could be explicitly obtained from one of the Pollaczek–Khintchine formulae (4.2.4), (4.2.7)–(4.2.9). A generalization of the Pollaczek–Khintchine formulae which allows jobs initiating the server from idle to have different service characteristics leads to the generalized Pollaczek–Khintchine formulae; the mean waiting time for such a system is given in (4.2.11), from which the mean number of jobs in the system and related measures could be obtained by application of Little's formulae. This generalization is especially useful for analyzing I/O devices and facilities with finite set-up delay.

The performance of the M/G/1 system is affected by the coefficients of variation of both the inter-arrival time and the service time; in either case, a low value for the coefficient of variation is generally preferred. Apart from the FIFO rule, the Pollaczek–Khintchine formulae will also give the right answers for rules which are non-preemptive and requirement independent.

4.7 Appendix 4A: The Mean Residual Service Delay Relating to the Pollaczek–Khintchine Formula

We shall first consider the service time distribution relating to the job in service as observed by a randomly arriving job. This distribution will in general be different from that of the ordinary service time because it is length-biased: arrival is less likely to occur during a short service than a long one. Thus the probability of encountering a service time of length x is proportional not only to the abundance or frequency of occurrence of such service times but also to the length x. If $f(x)$ denotes the probability density function of the ordinary service time, and $h(x)$, that of the service time as encountered by an arrival, then $h(x) \propto xf(x)$; or denoting the constant of proportionality by c, we have $h(x) = cxf(x)$. Since $h(x)$ must integrate to one, we must have

$$\int_0^\infty cxf(x)\,\mathrm{d}x = c\bar{X} = 1,$$

which implies $c = 1/\bar{X}$. Thus the mean service time as observed by an arrival is

$$\int_0^\infty xh(x)\mathrm{d}x = c\int_0^\infty x^2f(x)\,\mathrm{d}x = \overline{X^2}/\bar{X}$$

which is the total mean service time of the job in service as encountered by an arrival. Since a random arrival can occur anywhere in a service interval with equal probability, on average it would arrive midway in the interval so that the mean residual service time is

$$\tfrac{1}{2}\overline{X^2}/\bar{X}.$$

Now, residual service delay is applicable only when the server is found to be busy on arrival, and is not incurred if it is found to be idle; since the probability that the server is busy is $\rho = \lambda\bar{X}$, the mean residual service delay is therefore

$$\bar{S} = \rho[\tfrac{1}{2}\overline{X^2}/\bar{X}] + (1 - \rho) \times 0 = \tfrac{1}{2}\lambda\overline{X^2}.$$

By similar arguments, if there are p types of jobs in the system each with arrival rate λ_i and mean service time $\bar{X}_i$, the mean residual service delay is

$$\bar{S} = \tfrac{1}{2}\sum_{k=1}^{p}\lambda_k\overline{X_k^2}. \quad \square$$

4.8 Appendix 4B: The Mean Residual Service Delay Relating to the Generalized Pollaczek–Khintchine Formula

Letting ρ denote the server utilization in this situation, then the service time Z is

$$Z = \begin{cases} X & \text{with probability } \rho \\ Y & \text{with probability } 1 - \rho \end{cases}$$

The mean residual service delay $\bar{S}$ in this case, analogous to that for the Pollaczek–Khintchine formula, is

$$\tfrac{1}{2}\lambda\overline{Z^2}.$$

Thus we have

$$\bar{S} = \tfrac{1}{2}\lambda[\rho\overline{X^2} + (1 - \rho)\overline{Y^2}].$$

The mean service time is

$$\bar{Z} = \rho\bar{X} + (1 - \rho)\bar{Y}.$$

Multiplying both sides of the above by λ and noting that the utilization ρ is $\lambda\bar{Z}$, we can then solve for ρ; this gives $\rho = \lambda\bar{Y}/[1 - \lambda(\bar{X} - \bar{Y})]$. $\quad\nabla$

4.9 Exercises

1. The mean number of jobs enqueued to a particular I/O device (excluding the one in service) is observed to be 6.5, and the mean number of jobs in the system is 7.2. Given that the job arrival rate is 0.5/second determine the mean service time and the mean response time.

2. A communications line transmits fixed-length messages which arrive in accordance with a Poisson process. Suppose it is observed that the average number of messages awaiting transmission (excluding the one being transmitted) is $\bar{Q}$. Show that the line utilization is $\sqrt{[\bar{Q}^2 + 2\bar{Q}]} - \bar{Q}$.

3. Consider a situation similar to that in the previous exercise. Suppose here the message length is exponentially distributed, and that the mean number of messages in the system is given to be $\bar{J}$. Show that the line utilization is $\bar{J}/(\bar{J} + 1)$.

4. The coefficient of variation of the inter-arrival time of jobs entering a single processor system is found to be ≈ 0.9 and that of the service time is 0.5. Given that the processor utilization is 60%, estimate the mean number of jobs in the system. Is this an under-estimation or over-estimation?

5. (*Fixed Head Disk Processing*) The time taken to process a record on a fixed head disk unit consists of a rotational delay and a data transfer time. Suppose the rotational delay is uniformly distributed between 0 and 10 ms, and that the data transfer time is independent of the rotational delay and has mean and variance equal to 5 ms and 4 respectively. If request arrivals conform to a Poisson process with rate 30/second, calculate the mean request response

48

time. (*Note.* Since the records are of variable length, you may assume that the service requirements of initiators and non-initiators are identical.)

6. (*Fixed Head Disk Processing With Write Verification*) Consider the processing of records on a fixed head disk unit as in the previous exercise. Here we shall distinguish between the processing times of read and write requests. The processing time of read requests simply consists of a rotational delay and a data transfer time. For write requests, an additional delay of *write verification* to ensure that data are written on the disk correctly is required. Write verification consists of reading back the data just written and adds a further revolution to the service time compared with that for read requests. Supposing 10% of all requests require write verification, determine the mean response time for this situation. Does it differ significantly from that in the previous exercise?

7. Transactions arrive for processing at a particular device in accordance with a Poisson process with rate λ. The service time of these transactions is exponentially distributed. Suppose it is possible to combine several transactions, say n (a fixed number), together to form a single larger transaction, and that it is possible to regulate the resultant arrival behaviour so that these larger transactions, too, enter the system in a Poisson stream with rate λ/n. The service time of these larger transactions is the sum of those of the constituent transactions. Show that the mean waiting time of a larger transaction differs from that of an original transaction by a factor of $\frac{1}{2}(n+1)$.

8. Suppose jobs initiating a particular facility from idle incur an extra service overhead of 10% compared with other jobs. Suppose that the mean service time for initiators is 75 seconds, and that arrival is Poisson with rate 0.5/minute. Determine the mean service time and utilization of the device. What are the errors if we ignore the 10% overhead for initiators?

9. The utilization of a processor is found to be 30% and it is known that the coefficient of variation of the service time lies between 0.4 and 0.7. Given that job arrivals conform to a Poisson process, provide an estimate of the mean number of jobs in the system. What is the maximum error of this estimate?

10. Requests arrive for processing at a particular device in a Poisson manner at a traffic intensity of 70 second/second. It is observed that the service time is highly irregular—more so than that in the exponential case. Derive a lower bound on the mean number of jobs in the system.

11. A file enquiry system makes use of a sequential file of 10 000 records. Each enquiry requires information from a single record which is equally likely to be in any position in the file. In order to pinpoint the required record, the file is read from the beginning until it is found. Assuming the time taken to read a record from the file is constant and equals 10 ms and that enquiries arrive at the rate of 1 per minute in a Poisson manner, determine the average amount of time taken to answer an enquiry.

12. Consider the file enquiry system in the previous exercise. Suppose the mean response time there is considered to be too high. One method of improvement is to duplicate the entire file so that the workload to any one file is halved. Is the resultant response time halved? Is the improvement worthwhile?

13. The mean arrival and service rates of a single server system are respectively 20 and 34 jobs/second. The scheduling rule is such that when there are n jobs in the queue, each of them is randomly picked for service with the same probability $1/n$ irrespective of their arrival time. Given that both the inter-arrival and service times are exponentially distributed, determine the mean response time.

14. Consider a single server system in which the scheduling rule is such that the server alternates between the FIFO and LIFO rules whenever it dequeues a job for service. Given that the input is Poisson and that the service time is constant, calculate the mean normalized waiting time if the traffic intensity is 60%.

CHAPTER 5

Systems with Service Discriminations

5.1 Introduction

In this chapter, we shall look at systems with unequal treatment extended to different jobs. The commonest of such treatment is to attach a priority to different classes of jobs; priority scheduling is quite common in computer installations because generally not all jobs run in the installation are of equal importance. Production jobs, for example, are often more critical than development jobs and therefore have a higher priority assigned to them. In Sections 5.2 and 5.3 we shall look at two simple priority rules: non-preemptive and preemptive resume. In the former case, preferential treatment given to high-priority jobs is only applied at job completion times so that once a job commences execution, it continues without interruption to completion. In the latter case, a job in service can be interrupted by an arriving one which has a higher priority, and when the interrupted job eventually returns to service, resumption takes place from where it previously left off. When priority is assigned on the basis of job duration and where shorter jobs are given higher priority, we have the shortest-job-first discipline; this forms the subject of Section 5.4. Round-robin scheduling, a preemptive rule widely implemented in time-sharing systems, is examined in Section 5.5; it aims to allocate processor time evenly to all jobs present, but invariably discriminates against long ones and favours short ones.

5.2 Non-preemptive Priority Systems

Here we consider a situation where jobs coming into the system are divided into p priority classes. Each job has a priority index i ($1 \leqslant i \leqslant p$) associated with it. A job belonging to class i has a higher priority than those with index $i + 1, i + 2, \ldots, p$; but it has a lower priority than jobs with index $1, 2, \ldots, i - 1$. Hence the highest priority jobs are those with index 1, and the lowest priority jobs are those with index p. All executions, once started, are assumed to run to completion. When the processor completes a job, it selects for processing a job in the queue with the lowest index, and jobs belonging to the same class are processed in arrival sequence. Job arrivals in each class are assumed to conform to an independent Poisson process. For class i jobs, the average arrival rate is denoted by λ_i and the associated processing time is

50

denoted by X_i. The total arrival rate $\lambda_1 + \cdots + \lambda_p$ will be denoted by λ; we note that the aggregate arrival stream which results from merging together the p streams, as explained in Section 2.4, is also a Poisson stream.

5.2.1 The Mean Waiting Time

For an arriving job with arbitrary index i, we would like to determine its mean waiting time $\bar{W}_i$ by following its progress through the system; here $\bar{W}_i$ may be decomposed into three distinct parts:

(1) $\bar{S}$, the mean residual processing time of any job whose execution is in progress when the present class i job arrives;

(2) B, the mean total processing times of jobs of priority 1 through i which arrives before the present class i job;

(3) D, the mean total processing times of jobs of priority 1 through $i - 1$ which arrive after the present class i job but before it commences execution.

Thus the mean waiting time of a class i job can be written as

$$\bar{W}_i = \bar{S} + D + B. \tag{5.2.1}$$

As shown in Appendix 4A, the mean residual service delay $\bar{S}$ for multiple job classes is

$$\bar{S} = \tfrac{1}{2} \sum_{k=1}^{p} \lambda_k \overline{X_k^2}. \tag{5.2.2}$$

If $\bar{Q}_k$ signifies the average number of class k jobs in the queue (excluding the one in service), then B can be written as

$$B = \sum_{k=1}^{i} \bar{Q}_k \bar{X}_k. \tag{5.2.3}$$

Since from Little's formula, $\bar{Q}_k = \lambda_k \bar{W}_k$, this becomes

$$B = \sum_{k=1}^{i} \rho_k \bar{W}_k, \tag{5.2.4}$$

where $\rho_k = \lambda_k \bar{X}_k$ represents the average amount of work brought into the system per second by class k jobs. Next, the number of class k arrivals during the waiting time of the present class i job on average is $\lambda_k \bar{W}_i$, each of which would require an average processing time of $\bar{X}_k$. The total average processing requirements of these class k arrivals is therefore $\rho_k \bar{W}_i$. Since only those jobs with priority index less than i could delay the execution of the present job, we therefore have

$$D = \bar{W}_i \sum_{0 < k < i} \rho_k. \tag{5.2.5}$$

Hence substituting (5.2.4) and (5.2.5) into (5.2.1) we obtain

$$\bar{W}_i = [\bar{S} + \sum_{k=1}^{i} \rho_k \bar{W}_k]/[1 - \sum_{0 < k < i} \rho_k].$$

This is a set of equations involving i unknowns $\bar{W}_1, \ldots, \bar{W}_i$ which can be solved successively (i.e. solving for $\bar{W}_1$ first and then $\bar{W}_2$ and so on) to yield

$$\bar{W}_i = \bar{S}/[(1 - U_i)(1 - U_{i-1})] \tag{5.2.6}$$

where $U_0 = 0$, and $U_i = \Sigma_{k=1}^{i} \rho_k$, $i > 0$, is the cumulative utilization caused by jobs with priority index $\leq i$. Expanding $\bar{S}$ using (5.2.2), we have

$$\bar{W}_i = \frac{\frac{1}{2} \sum_{k=1}^{p} \lambda_k \overline{X_k^2}}{(1 - U_i)(1 - U_{i-1})}. \tag{5.2.7}$$

Equation (5.2.7), of course, gives the the mean waiting time relating to class i jobs only. The overall mean waiting time $\bar{W}$ can be obtained as follows. Let $\bar{Q}$ be the mean total number of jobs in the queue, and $\bar{Q}_k$ be the mean number of class k jobs in the queue. Then

$$\bar{Q} = \bar{Q}_1 + \bar{Q}_2 + \cdots + \bar{Q}_p.$$

But from Little's formula, $\bar{Q} = \lambda \bar{W}$ and $\bar{Q}_k = \lambda_k \bar{W}_k$; making these substitutions, we obtain

$$\bar{W} = \sum_{k=1}^{p} \lambda_k \bar{W}_k/\lambda. \tag{5.2.8}$$

Thus we see that the overall waiting time is simply the weighted sum of all the waiting times of the individual classes, with weighting factor equal to the fraction of arrivals relating to that class. By the same token, the overall average response time $\bar{R}$ is

$$\bar{R} = \sum_{k=1}^{p} \lambda_k (\bar{W}_k + \bar{X}_k)/\lambda. \tag{5.2.9}$$

Example 5.1 A computer manager is planning to introduce a priority system in the processing of jobs in the installation. All jobs in the installation possess the following processing characteristics: the mean processing requirement is 10 ms, and the corresponding second moment is 120. The manager is considering dividing the jobs into five priority classes of equal size. Supposing there is an average of 10 arrivals/second from each class and that arrivals follow a Poisson stream, calculate (a) the mean waiting time for each job class, (b) the overall mean waiting time.

Solution. Since the class arrival rate for each class is the same and equals 0.01/ms, we have from (5.2.2), the mean residual processing time

$$\bar{S} = \tfrac{1}{2}[5 \times 0.01 \times 120] = 3 \text{ ms.}$$

Since $\rho_i = 0.01 \times 10 = 0.1$ for all i, we have $U_1 = 0.1; U_2 = 0.2; U_3 = 0.3; U_4 = 0.4; U_5 = 0.5$. From (5.2.6), the mean waiting time for the different job classes are

$$\bar{W}_1 = 3/0.9 = 3.33 \text{ ms;}$$
$$\bar{W}_2 = 3/(0.8 \times 0.9) = 4.17 \text{ ms;}$$
$$\bar{W}_3 = 3/(0.7 \times 0.8) = 5.36 \text{ ms;}$$
$$\bar{W}_4 = 3/(0.6 \times 0.7) = 7.14 \text{ ms;}$$
$$\bar{W}_5 = 3/(0.5 \times 0.6) = 10.0 \text{ ms.}$$

The overall mean waiting time is, from (5.2.8),

$$(3.33 + 4.17 + 5.36 + 7.14 + 10.0)/5 = 6 \text{ ms.}$$

We see that jobs belonging to classes 1, 2, and 3 would have above average performance but the opposite is true for jobs belonging to classes 4 and 5. For class 5 jobs, there is a 67% degradation, while for class 1 jobs there is an improvement of 45%. We also note that, although there is not a vast difference (< 1 ms) in the mean waiting time between class 1 and class 2 jobs, the corresponding difference between class 4 and class 5 jobs (nearly 3 ms) is much more pronounced. □

Example 5.2 A communications line is responsible for transmitting two types of fixed length messages. The message arrival pattern is Poisson and the transmission times of these two types of messages are 0.5 second and 1 second respectively. Suppose the total message arrival rate is 1/second, and that the short messages make up 80% of the total traffic. Compare the operation of a non-preemptive system with priority given to short messages and that of a system with the priorities reversed.

Solution. The mean residual transmission time $\bar{S}$, from (5.2.2), is

$$0.5(0.8 \times 0.5^2 + 0.2 \times 1^2) = 0.2 \text{ second.}$$

First, we consider a system with priority given to short messages, which we shall call Scheme 1; then

$$U_1 = 0.8 \times 0.5 = 0.4$$
$$U_2 = 0.8 \times 0.5 + 0.2 \times 1 = 0.6.$$

From (5.2.6), we obtain

$$\bar{W}_1 = 0.2/(1 - 0.4) = 0.33 \text{ second}$$
$$\bar{W}_2 = 0.2/[(1 - 0.4)(1 - 0.6)] = 0.83 \text{ second}.$$

The corresponding mean response times are therefore

$$\bar{R}_1 = 0.33 + 0.5 = 0.83 \text{ second}$$
$$\bar{R}_2 = 0.83 + 1 = 1.83 \text{ seconds},$$

giving an overall mean response time of

$$\bar{R} = 0.8 \times 0.83 + 0.2 \times 1.83 = 1.03 \text{ seconds}.$$

If we reverse the priorities—we shall call this Scheme 2—we have the following cumulative utilizations

$$U'_1 = 0.2$$
$$U'_2 = 0.6,$$

so that the corresponding mean waiting times are

$$\bar{W}'_1 = 0.2/(1 - 0.2) = 0.25 \text{ second}$$
$$\bar{W}'_2 = 0.2/[(1 - 0.6)(1 - 0.2)] = 0.63 \text{ second}.$$

The corresponding mean response times are therefore

$$\bar{R}'_1 = 1.25 \text{ seconds}$$
$$\bar{R}'_2 = 1.13 \text{ seconds},$$

giving an overall mean response time of

$$\bar{R}' = 0.8 \times 1.13 + 0.2 \times 1.25 = 1.15 \text{ seconds}.$$

We see that Scheme 1 gives better overall performance than Scheme 2 and results in an improvement in overall mean response time of 10.4%. The difference in mean response time between the two message types is much greater in Scheme 1 than in Scheme 2. In Scheme 2, there is only a slight difference in the mean response time between the long and short messages in spite of the half a second difference in their transmission time; in Scheme 1, this difference is 1 second—which may or may not be acceptable, depending on the relative urgency of the two message types (see Example 5.5 below). Compared with Scheme 1, the mean response time for long messages in Scheme 2 is improved by 31.7%; this is done at the expense of the short messages, whose mean response time is degraded by 36.1%. □

5.2.2 Invariance Property

At the end of the previous chapter, we examined an invariance property relating to systems in which there is only a single job class. A similar property in fact holds also in the case of multiple job classes: for a conservative, non-preemptive system with p job classes each with traffic intensity ρ_k, and if $\bar{W}_k$ denotes the mean waiting time of class k jobs, then the weighted sum

$$\sum_{k=1}^{p} \rho_k \bar{W}_k, \qquad (5.2.10)$$

is invariant with respect to the (non-preemptive) scheduling rule; this invariance holds for any single server system with arbitrary arrival and service characteristics. (A proof of this in the case of Poisson arrival may be found in Kleinrock (1976).) Intuitively, the invariance of (5.2.10) says that if special treatment is extended to one particular class of jobs, it can only be achieved at the expense of other classes so that the sum (5.2.10) remains constant. The following two examples illustrate these ideas.

Example 5.3 Jobs arrive at a particular facility for processing in accordance with a Poisson process at a rate of 10 jobs/minute. All jobs have the same service characteristics: the service time is exponentially distributed with a mean of 4 seconds. Calculate the overall mean waiting time for the following situations: (a) the jobs are divided into two priority classes of equal size (with Poisson arrival assumed for each class); (b) the jobs are divided into five priority classes of equal size (with Poisson arrival assumed for each class); (c) no priorities are distinguished among jobs.

Solution. Suppose the jobs are divided into p classes each with Poisson arrival. The class arrival rates are the same and equal $10/p$ jobs/minute, and the mean service time, too, is the same for all classes and equals $\frac{1}{15}$ minute. Substituting these into (5.2.10), we have

$$\sum_{k=1}^{p} (10/p)\bar{W}_k/15.$$

In the special case $p = 1$ (i.e. no priorities), the mean waiting time obtained from the Pollaczek–Khintchine formula is

$$(10/15^2)/(1 - \tfrac{10}{15}) = \tfrac{2}{15} \text{ minute.}$$

Substituting this into (5.2.10) gives $20/15^2$. By invariance, this should be the same as the corresponding expression for general p above. Equating the two, we conclude that the mean waiting time when there are p classes is

$$\sum_{k=1}^{p} \lambda_k \bar{W}_k/\lambda \sum_{k=1}^{p} \bar{W}_k/p = \tfrac{2}{15} \text{ minute.}$$

Thus, the answers to (a), (b), and (c) are the same and equal 8 seconds. □

Example 5.4 A computer system processes two types of jobs: type 1 has a traffic intensity of 0.2, and type 2 has a traffic intensity of 0.5, with non-preemptive priority given to type 1 jobs. The system manager, however, wishes to investigate the effect of swapping the job priorities; an effect of the swapping is that the mean waiting time of type 1 jobs is found to reduce by 90 seconds. Determine the corresponding change in the mean waiting time of type 2 jobs.

Solution. Before the priorities are swapped, the quantity corresponding to (5.2.10) is

$$0.2\bar{W}_1 + 0.5\bar{W}_2.$$

If $\bar{W}_1'$ and $\bar{W}_2'$ respectively denote the mean waiting time of type 1 and type 2 jobs after the priorities are swapped, we have, by invariance,

$$0.2\bar{W}_1 + 0.5\bar{W}_2 = 0.2\bar{W}_1' + 0.5\bar{W}_2'.$$

This means

$$\bar{W}_2' - \bar{W}_2 = -0.2(\bar{W}_1' - \bar{W}_1)/0.5.$$

Since $(\bar{W}_1' - \bar{W}_1)$ is given to be -90 seconds, we therefore conclude that the mean waiting time for type 2 jobs is increased by 36 seconds as a result of the swap. $\square$

5.2.3 Optimal Priority Assignment

In the evaluation of the waiting time in Section 5.2.1, we presuppose that priority classes have already been assigned to different types of jobs, each identified by its processing requirement. In this section, we shall consider how priority should be assigned to different classes of jobs given their processing requirements and a measure of their relative importance.

Suppose the importance of a job is measured by a cost or weight attached to each second the job waits in the system: we denote by $\bar{V}_k$ the average cost of keeping a job of type k waiting for one second. If $\bar{W}_k$ signifies the average waiting time (excluding service) of type k jobs, and if the associated job arrival is Poisson with rate λ_k, then the mean waiting cost $\bar{V}$ incurred by the system per second is the mean number of job arrivals per second times the mean waiting cost associated with each arrival:

$$\bar{V} = \sum_{k=1}^{p} \lambda_k \bar{V}_k \bar{W}_k.$$

For an optimal priority assignment with minimum cost $\bar{V}^*$, interchanging the priority of any two neighbouring classes necessarily yields a different cost $\bar{V}'$ such that $\bar{V}' \geqslant \bar{V}^*$. From this line of reasoning, it can be shown (see Cox and

Smith (1961)) that the necessary condition for optimal priority assignment is the following:

$$\bar{X}_1/\bar{V}_1 \leqslant \bar{X}_2/\bar{V}_2 \leqslant \cdots \leqslant \bar{X}_p/\bar{V}_p. \tag{5.2.11}$$

This means that the job type with the lowest mean processing time to cost ratio should be assigned top priority, and the job type with the next lowest ratio should be assigned the next priority and so on. Intuitively, (5.2.11) suggests that the priority index of a job type should be inversely proportional to its importance and directly proportional to its mean processing requirement. In the special case where all jobs are of equal importance (i.e. all V_i's are the same), then (5.2.11) reduces to

$$\bar{X}_1 \leqslant \bar{X}_2 \leqslant \cdots \leqslant \bar{X}_p, \tag{5.2.12}$$

which means that short jobs should be given priority treatment over long ones for optimal performance.

Example 5.5 Consider the message transmission system in Example 5.2. Suppose there is an urgency factor associated with the message types. Determine the optimal priority assignment if (a) the long messages are five times more urgent than the short ones, (b) the long messages are twice as urgent as the short ones, and (c) both types of messages are equally urgent.

Solution. For (a), the mean processing time to cost (here the waiting cost is taken to be the urgency factor) ratios for the long and short messages respectively are $1/5$ and $0.5/1$. Thus from (5.2.11), the long messages should have priority over the short ones. For (b), the corresponding ratios are $1/2$ and 0.5 respectively; since they are the same, this means that priority given to either type would be equally effective. For (c), since both types of messages are equally urgent, (5.2.12) implies that priority should be given to the short messages. $\square$

5.3 Preemptive Resume Priority Systems

Here, as in Section 5.2, we consider jobs distinguishable into p priority classes, and we shall adopt the same notations as in that section. In the present system, however, an arriving job having a lower priority index than the job being executed immediately obtains processor attention, thereby interrupting the execution of the job in service. When the latter job eventually returns to service, its execution is resumed from where it left off with no loss of earlier service. We shall concentrate on the mean response time $\bar{R}_i$ of a class i job. In this situation, $\bar{R}_i$ could be broken down into three components:

(1) H, the average amount of work already present in the system—sometimes called the unfinished work—relating to classes 1 through i, all of which have to be processed before the present class i job commences service;

Table 5.1

Tasks	Average processing time (ms)	Arrival rate (per ms)	Priority index
1	0.4	0.5	1
2	0.1	3.0	2
3	1.5	0.2	3

(2) P, the average delay caused by jobs with priority index 1 through $i - 1$ entering the system after the arrival of the present class i job but before its processing is completed;

(3) $\bar{X}_i$, its own mean execution time.

That is

$$\bar{R}_i = H + P + \bar{X}_i. \tag{5.3.1}$$

In Appendix 5A, it is shown that

$$H = \tfrac{1}{2} \sum_{k=1}^{i} \lambda_k \overline{X_k^2}/(1 - U_i). \tag{5.3.2}$$

The component P is similar to the quantity D in Section 5.2.1 except that high-priority arrivals during the execution of the present job could also delay its progress to completion; analogously to (5.2.5), we have

$$P = \sum_{0<k<i} \lambda_k \bar{X}_k \bar{R}_i = \bar{R}_i U_{i-1}. \tag{5.3.3}$$

Substituting (5.3.2), (5.3.3) into (5.3.1) and rearranging, we obtain

$$\bar{R}_i = \frac{\bar{X}_i}{1 - U_{i-1}} + \frac{\tfrac{1}{2} \sum_{k=1}^{i} \lambda_k \overline{X_k^2}}{(1 - U_i)(1 - U_{i-1})}. \tag{5.3.4}$$

The overall average response time $\bar{R}$, similar to that in the non-preemptive case, is

$$\bar{R} = \sum_{k=1}^{p} \lambda_k \bar{R}_k/\lambda. \tag{5.3.5}$$

Example 5.6 (Interrupt Processing). A CPU supports three types of tasks with characteristics given in Table 5.1. The system is a preemptive priority one in which a high-priority task is allowed to interrupt the processing of a lower-priority task. Supposing both the inter-arrival time and processing time are exponentially distributed, determine the mean response time for each type of task. What would be the effect if interrupts were disabled?

Solution. Here we have the cumulative utilizations

$$U_1 = 0.2$$
$$U_2 = 0.2 + 0.3 = 0.5$$
$$U_3 = 0.5 + 0.3 = 0.8.$$

From (2.2.3), the second moments of the three types of tasks are found to be respectively 0.32, 0.02, and 4.5. Substituting these and the given parameters into (5.3.4), we obtain

$$\bar{R}_1 = 0.4 + 0.5(0.5 \times 0.32)/0.8 = 0.5 \text{ ms}$$
$$\bar{R}_2 = 0.1/0.8 + 0.5(0.5 \times 0.32 + 3 \times 0.02)/(0.8 \times 0.5) = 0.4 \text{ ms}$$
$$\bar{R}_3 = 1.5/0.5 + 0.5(0.5 \times 0.32 + 3 \times 0.02 + 0.2 \times 4.5)/(0.2 \times 0.5) = 8.6 \text{ ms}.$$

The overall mean response time is

$$\bar{R} = (0.5 \times 0.5 + 3 \times 0.4 + 0.2 \times 8.6)/3.7 = 0.86 \text{ ms}.$$

If interrupts are disabled, then from (5.2.7) and incorporating the relevant service times, we obtain the following mean response time for the relevant tasks

$$\bar{R}'_1 = 1.1 \text{ ms}$$
$$\bar{R}'_2 = 1.5 \text{ ms}$$
$$\bar{R}'_3 = 7.1 \text{ ms}.$$

The overall mean response time is thus

$$\bar{R}' = 1.75 \text{ ms}.$$

Thus, the overall performance is much better if interrupts are enabled: this gives a reduction of 50.9% in the overall mean response time. The mean response time for type 1 tasks, too, suffers substantial degradation if interrupts are disabled: the mean response time for type 1 tasks is increased by a factor of 2.2 and that for type 2 tasks is increased by a factor of 3.75. In fact, type 2 tasks seem to suffer most because their mean processing requirement is only 0.1 ms—this gives a normalized mean response time of $1.5/0.1 = 15$. The only tasks that stand to gain from disabling the interrupt mechanism are type 3 tasks, whose mean requirement is much larger than those of other types. The overall performance degradation resulting from disabling the interrupt mechanism seems to largely come from the residual service delay of these long tasks. □

5.4 The Shortest-job-first Rule

In the non-preemptive priority system, different job classes are identified by their processing requirements, and priority can thus be regarded as being assigned on the basis of the processing requirement. In the case of the shortest-job-first (SJF) rule, selection is based solely on job duration. When the processor completes a job, the shortest job in the queue is selected for execution, and once execution has started, it continues to completion. In fact, the results for the SJF rule can be obtained as a direct extension of those relating to the non-preemptive system.

Suppose we denote the probability density function of the processing time by $f(x)$ and we divide jobs into an infinite number of classes according to their duration: jobs having a processing requirement in the range $I(x) = [x, x + dx)$ are grouped into the same class. Thus instead of having a discrete priority index, we have a continuous one, and for $x < y$, jobs in class $I(x)$ have precedence over those in class $I(y)$. The proportion of jobs falling into the class $I(x)$ is $f(x) dx$ with class arrival rate $\lambda f(x)dx$, where λ is the overall arrival rate, and their processing time is simply constant and equals x. Hence, on suitably replacing summation over the discrete priority index k by integration over the continuous index x, we obtain from (5.2.7) the mean waiting time $\bar{W}(t)$ for a job with processing requirement t under the SJF rule:

$$\bar{W}(t) = \tfrac{1}{2}\lambda\overline{X^2}/[1 - U(t)]^2, \tag{5.4.1}$$

where

$$U(t) = \lambda \int_0^t xf(x)\,dx,$$

is the cumulative utilization of the processor caused by jobs having a processing requirement $\leqslant t$, since $\lambda f(x) dx$ gives the arrival rate of jobs having a processing time of x. Evidently, as $t \to \infty$, we have $U(t) \to \rho$. In terms of the coefficient of variation, (5.4.1) can be written as

$$\bar{W}(t) = \tfrac{1}{2}\rho\bar{X}[1 + C(X)^2]/[1 - U(t)]^2; \tag{5.4.2}$$

this is often referred to as *Phipps' formula* and it was first demonstrated in Phipps (1961). It is interesting to note that for very short jobs with processing requirement $t \to 0$ (these are those receiving the most favourable treatment) their mean waiting time is

$$\bar{W}(0) = \tfrac{1}{2}\rho\bar{X}[1 + C(X)^2];$$

this is shorter than that obtained from the Pollaczek–Khintchine formula which differs from $\bar{W}(0)$ by the factor $1/(1 - \rho)$. Likewise, for very long jobs with processing requirement $t \to \infty$ (these are those receiving the most unfavourable treatment) their mean waiting time is

$$\bar{W}(\infty) = \tfrac{1}{2}\rho\bar{X}[1 + C(X)^2]/(1 - \rho)^2.$$

This time is longer than that obtained from the Pollaczek–Khintchine formula and differs from that formula by the same factor $1/(1 - \rho)$. Thus if $\bar{W}$ signifies the mean waiting time calculated from the Pollaczek–Khintchine formula, we have for $0 < \rho < 1$

$$\bar{W}(0) < \bar{W} < \bar{W}(\infty). \tag{5.4.3}$$

We note that the factor $1/(1 - \rho)$ is approximately one for small utilization but diverges for high utilization. Equation (5.4.3) indicates that the FIFO rule, unlike the SJF rule, provides a generally 'fairer' and more uniform treatment to all jobs irrespective of their requirement. Such discrimination is hardly noticeable when utilization is low but could escalate to a significant degree when the utilization is high.

Example 5.7 A system designer faces a choice of adopting either the SJF rule or the FIFO rule. Suppose the processing requirement X of the jobs in question can be approximated by a uniform distribution over the interval $(0, T)$, and that the arrival stream is Poisson. It is considered that the SJF rule is worthwhile only if at least 75% of the jobs is better off under it. Determine whether the SJF rule should be adopted if the processor utilization is given to be 50%.

Solution. Let λ be the arrival rate; then the cumulative utilization for $t < T$ is

$$U(t) = \lambda \int_0^t x/T \, dx = \lambda t^2/(2T).$$

The processor utilization is $\rho = \lambda T/2$. From Section 2.3, the second moment of the processing time is $T^2/3$. Substituting these into (5.4.1) and simplifying, we have

$$\bar{W}(t) = 4\rho T^3/[3(2T - \lambda t^2)^2].$$

The corresponding mean waiting time $\bar{W}$ for the FIFO rule is, by the Pollaczek–Khintchine formula,

$$\bar{W} = \rho T/[3(1 - \rho)].$$

Thus the jobs which are better off under SJF are those with processing requirement t such that $\bar{W}(t) < \bar{W}$; i.e.

$$4\rho T^3/[3(2T - \lambda t^2)^2] < \rho T/[3(1 - \rho)].$$

This implies

$$t < T \sqrt{\{[1 - \sqrt{(1 - \rho)}]/\rho\}} = t^*.$$

Thus, the proportion of jobs better off under SJF is

$$\Pr[X < t^*] = t^*/T = \sqrt{\{[1 - \sqrt{(1 - \rho)}]/\rho\}},$$

which equals 76.5% for $\rho = 50\%$. Consequently, the SJF rule should be adopted according to the criterion given. $\square$

5.5 The Round-robin Rule

The round-robin (RR) rule is a preemptive rule which aims to provide a uniform treatment to all the jobs present in the system by limiting the amount of time that the processor is continuously allocated to any given job to a fixed amount of q units, called a *quantum*. In this system, a new arrival is placed at the end of the queue while the processor is allocated to the job at the head of the queue. When the processor is allocated to a job, it executes for a time of q time units, at the expiration of which the processing of the job is suspended. The processor would then turn its attention to the next job in the queue which will likewise be executed for a quantum. When a job completes a quantum of processing, its total service requirement is assumed to have been met in full—hence departing from the system—with probability $1 - p$ independent of the processing it has attained so far, but remains in the system to rejoin the end of the queue for further processing with probability p. Thus the probability that the processing requirement X of a job equals k quanta is given by

$$\Pr[X = kq] = p^{k-1}(1 - p), \qquad k = 1, 2, \ldots . \qquad (5.5.1)$$

That is, the processing time is geometrically distributed which, as explained in Chapter 2, is the discrete analogue of the exponential distribution and possesses the memoryless property; the average processing time is $\bar{X} = q/(1 - p)$, and the mean number of quanta required by a job is $1/(1 - p)$. Although the processor gives the same treatment to all jobs present in the system, short jobs will invariably benefit from this scheme because their completion rate is higher and they do not need to wait for the processing requirements of earlier jobs to be met in full before they can receive processor attention. Its preemptive character also means that the progress of a job through the system could be delayed by that of a subsequently arriving one. Under Poisson input with rate λ, it is shown in Kleinrock (1967) that the mean response time $\bar{R}_i$ for a job requiring i quanta of service is

$$\bar{R}_i = \bar{R}_1 + (i - 1)q/(1 - \rho) + q[\lambda \bar{R}_1 + p\bar{J} - \rho/(1 - \rho)](1 - a^{i-1})/(1 - a), \qquad (5.5.2)$$

where ρ is the utilization factor $\lambda q/(1 - p)$; $a = \lambda q + p$; $\bar{J}$ is the mean number of jobs in the system (which, in fact, coincides with that under the FIFO rule):

$$\bar{J} = \rho + (1 + p)\rho^2/[2(1 - \rho)], \qquad (5.5.3)$$

and $\bar{R}_1$ is given by $(1 - \rho)q/2 + \bar{J}q$. Although (5.5.2) is rather complicated, it is shown in Kleinrock (1964) that a good approximation is

$$\bar{R}_i \simeq iq\bar{J} + iq. \qquad (5.5.4)$$

This can be seen intuitively by noting that a job requiring i quanta must queue i times. Since the average number of jobs in the system is $\bar{J}$, its waiting time for each pass is thus $\bar{J}q$, which coupled with its processing requirement iq immediately gives (5.5.4). In the case of the FIFO rule, the average waiting time of a job is $\bar{J}\bar{X}$, and for a job requiring i quanta, its exact average response time $\bar{R}_i'$ is

$$\bar{R}_i' = \bar{J}\bar{X} + iq. \tag{5.5.5}$$

Comparing (5.5.4) and (5.5.5), we see that any job whose processing requirement iq exceeds $\bar{X}$ will be better off under FIFO scheduling but those with processing requirement below $\bar{X}$ will be better off under RR scheduling. The approximate proportion of jobs which are better off under FIFO scheduling is the sum $\Sigma\Pr[X = kq]$ over the set of values k where $kq > \bar{X}$, or $k \geqslant \lceil 1/(1-p)\rceil$; from (5.5.1), this proportion is

$$\Pr[X > \bar{X}] = p^{\{\lceil 1/(1-p)\rceil - 1\}}. \tag{5.5.6}$$

Example 5.8 In a time-sharing system, suppose it is given that the processing requirement is geometrically distributed with an average of 2.5 quanta. It is considered that the implementation of the RR rule is worthwhile only if 90% of the jobs are better off under it. Determine whether the RR rule should be implemented in this situation. What if the criterion is altered to 80% of the jobs are better off under the RR rule?

Solution. We are given that $1/(1-p) = 2.5$ so that $p = 0.6$. Substituting this value into (5.5.6), we find the proportion of jobs better off under FIFO to be

$$0.6^2 = 36\%.$$

Thus the proportion of jobs better off under RR is 64%. Since this is less than 90%, the RR rule should not be implemented. Even if the proportion is lowered to 80%, the RR rule should not be adopted. □

5.6 The Processor Sharing Rule

Next, we consider a continuous analogue of the RR system. Supposing, for a fixed mean processing requirement, we shrink the quantum size to zero while keeping the mean processing requirement $\bar{X}$ (and hence ρ) constant; then $p = 1 - q/\bar{X} \to 1$. The corresponding processing time distribution, as explained in Chapter 2, would then approach the exponential distribution. The mean number of jobs in the system, from (5.5.3), would approach

$$\bar{J} = \rho + \rho^2/(1 - \rho). \tag{5.6.1}$$

Replacing the discrete processing requirement iq by the continuous requirement t in (5.5.4), we have for the average response time $\bar{R}(t)$ of a job with processing requirement t

$$\bar{R}(t) = (\bar{J} + 1)t = t/(1 - \rho). \tag{5.6.2}$$

This idealized situation corresponds to a system in which the processor is equally shared among all jobs present: when there are k jobs in the system, the processing demand of each job is cleared at the rate of $(1/k)$ second/second. Consequently, this rule is called the processor sharing (PS) rule. Furthermore, the number of jobs in the system can be shown (see Gelenbe and Mitrani (1980)) to conform to the geometric distribution: if p_k signifies the probability that there are k jobs in the system, then

$$p_k = (1 - \rho) \rho^k, \qquad k = 0, 1, \ldots . \qquad (5.6.3)$$

We remark that although (5.6.2) was derived only for the case of exponential processing time, it actually holds for arbitrary processing time distribution; a proof of this may be found in Kleinrock (1976). The overall response time averaging over all jobs under the PS scheme is

$$\bar{R} = \overline{R(X)} = \int_0^\infty \bar{R}(t) f(t) \, dt,$$

where $f(t)$ is the probability density function of the processing time, and so

$$\bar{R} = \bar{X}/(1 - \rho). \qquad (5.6.4)$$

Comparing (5.6.2) and (5.6.4), we see that, similar to the RR rule,

$$\bar{R}(t) \begin{cases} < \bar{R} & \text{for } t < \bar{X} \\ > \bar{R} & \text{for } t > \bar{X}; \end{cases}$$

i.e. jobs having a below average processing requirement are treated favourably but those with above average requirement are discriminated against. If $F(t)$ denotes the cumulative distribution function of the processing time, then the proportion of jobs better off under PS is $\Pr[X < \bar{X}] = F(\bar{X})$.

We note that (5.6.4) is in general different from the mean response time obtained from the Pollaczek–Khintchine formula because the present system is a preemptive one—jobs requiring more than one quantum is always preempted—and so would not possess the invariance property. However, in the special case where the coefficient of variation of the service time $C(X) = 1$, (5.6.4) actually coincides with the mean response time given by the Pollaczek–Khintchine formula. Since, as we noted in Section 4.4, the mean response time of the M/G/1 queue is an increasing function of $C(X)$, this implies

$$\bar{R}_{\text{FIFO}} \begin{cases} < \bar{R}_{\text{PS}} & \text{if } C(X) < 1 \\ > \bar{R}_{\text{PS}} & \text{if } C(X) > 1, \end{cases}$$

where $\bar{R}_{\text{FIFO}}$ and $\bar{R}_{\text{PS}}$ represent the mean response times relating to the FIFO and PS rules respectively.

So far, we have ignored any overhead associated with the swapping from job to job. Swapping overhead, for example, may include the saving and loading of registers and program status information. It is not difficult to incorporate such swapping overhead in the case of the PS rule. If h signifies the fraction of time spent in each quantum in dealing with swapping activities, and if ρ^* signifies the resultant processor utilization with the swapping overhead included, then the relationship between ρ^* and the traffic intensity ρ (which is the processor utilization with the swapping overhead ignored) is

$$\rho^*(1 - h) = \rho,$$

so that the effective processor utilization is

$$\rho^* = \rho/(1 - h). \qquad (5.6.5)$$

Thus, on replacing ρ by ρ^* in (5.6.1)–(5.6.4), the swapping overhead could be incorporated.

Example 5.9 (Buffer Allocation). A time-sharing system operates the RR rule with a very small quantum size. The processing requirement of jobs is exponentially distributed; the job arrival stream is Poisson, and the traffic intensity is 0.6. Supposing the swapping overhead is 10%, determine the minimum buffer size for accommodating the jobs in the system given that no more than 5% of the jobs may overflow the buffer. What is the corresponding minimum buffer size if the swapping overhead is ignored?

Solution. Since the quantum size is assumed to be small, we may represent this situation by a PS system. From (5.6.5), the effective processor utilization is

$$\rho^* = 0.6/0.9 = \tfrac{2}{3}.$$

From (5.6.3), the probability that the number of jobs in the system $\geq x$ is

$$\sum_{k \geq x} p_k = (\rho^*)^x = (\tfrac{2}{3})^x.$$

Equating this with the maximum overflow probability of 5% and solving for x, we obtain the minimum buffer size

$$x \ln(\tfrac{2}{3}) = \ln(0.05),$$

which implies $x = 7.4$. Hence, the required minimum buffer size is 7.4 rounded up to the next integer, which is 8. If the swapping overhead is ignored, then the processor utilization is 0.6; carrying out the same calculations as above, we obtain $x = 5.9$, giving a minimum buffer size of 6. This indicates that ignoring the swapping overhead could result in a significant under-estimation of resource requirement. □

5.7 Summary

In this chapter, we have considered situations where unequal treatment is extended to different jobs; these jobs are generally distinguished either by their processing requirement or by their relative importance. Priority scheduling deals with multiple job classes with a priority index attached to each class. Non-preemptive priority scheduling allows no interruption of a job being executed by a higher-priority job; the key result for non-preemptive priority queues is the waiting time formula (5.2.7). Non-preemptive priority queues exhibit a certain degree of invariance: it is generally not possible to simultaneously reduce the mean waiting times of all job classes, and if the mean waiting time of a class is reduced, it is usually achieved at the expense of another; this fact is expressed more concisely in the invariance of (5.2.10). When non-preemptive priority is assigned on the basis of processing requirement with priority given to short jobs, then we have the SJF rule; the key result here is Phipps' formula (5.4.2). If the assignment of priority has not been made, then the criterion introduced in Section 5.2.3 could be used to effect optimal priority ordering based on the mean processing time and a measure of the relative importance of different job classes; this simple criterion suggests that priority should be assigned on the basis of the mean processing time to cost ratio, with top priority assigned to jobs with the smallest such ratio.

We have considered two main preemptive rules in this chapter: preemption based on priority, and preemption based on uniform sharing of resources. In the former, an arriving high priority job could demand immediate processor attention and interrupt the execution of a lower priority one; the key result here is the response time formula (5.3.4). The RR preemptive rule attempts to treat all jobs in the system in a uniform manner by limiting the amount of time—a quantum—the processor can be continuously allocated to a job. This rule invariably discriminates in favour of short jobs as their processing requirement could be met in full sooner than long ones. For finite quantum size, the key result for geometrically distributed processing requirement is the response time formula (5.5.2). When the quantum size approaches zero, the RR rule becomes the PS rule; the key result here, which is applicable to arbitrarily distributed processing requirement, is the response time formula (5.6.2).

5.8 Appendix 5A: The Average Unfinished Work

In a system where no work is created or destroyed, the average amount of unfinished work in the system is invariant with respect to the scheduling rule, which can be taken to be the mean waiting time in the M/G/1:CONS queue introduced in Section 4.5. Thus, analogous to (4.2.1), we have for the average unfinished work

$$H = \text{Mean Residual Service Time}/[1 - \text{Server Utilization}].$$

Here, since jobs belonging to class $> i$ are effectively invisible to class i jobs, the average residual service time, analogous to (5.2.2), is

$$\bar{S} = \tfrac{1}{2} \sum_{k=1}^{i} \lambda_k \overline{X_k^2}.$$

Likewise, the server utilization here as viewed by a class i job is U_i. Substituting these into the above expression for H, we obtain (5.3.2). ∇

Table 5.2

Message type	Average transmission time (seconds)	Arrival rate (per second)	Priority index
1	0.3	0.1	1
2	0.2	1.4	2
3	1.0	0.2	3
4	0.1	0.5	4

5.9 Exercises

1. Jobs arrive for processing at a data processing centre in a Poisson manner at an average rate of 7 jobs/hour. The mean and coefficient of variation of the processing requirement are 6 minutes and 0.7 respectively. Suppose 10% of these jobs are critical ones and that it is found that the current FIFO rule gives an unacceptably slow response for these jobs. However, it is considered that the adoption of a priority scheme giving top priority to these critical jobs is worthwhile only if the mean response time for these jobs can be improved by at least 20%. Determine whether non-preemptive priority scheduling should be implemented in this situation. Should the preemptive resume priority system be considered ?

2. A computer installation operates a non-preemptive priority system. There are three job types; the arrival of each type is Poisson with respective hourly arrival rates of 4, 7, and 15. Their processing times are exponentially distributed with respective mean values 4 minutes, 2 minutes, and 1 minute. Compare the operation of the following systems: (a) jobs with short mean processing time are given precedence over those with long mean processing time; (b) jobs with a low class arrival rate are given precedence over those with a high class arrival rate.

3. A computer system processes three types of jobs: type 1 has a traffic intensity of 0.1, type 2 has a traffic intensity of 0.2, and type 3 has a traffic intensity of 0.4. It operates a non-preemptive priority rule with top priority given to type 1 jobs, and bottom priority given to type 3 jobs. In an experiment aimed to re-designate priorities, the mean waiting time of type 3 jobs is found to improve by 10 seconds, and that of type 1 job is found to degrade by 6 seconds. Determine the corresponding change in the mean waiting time of type 2 jobs.

4. A communications line operates the non-preemptive priority rule and accepts input from four Poisson message sources. The characteristics of the associated messages are given in Table 5.2. Determine the mean residual transmission delay as observed by an arriving message if (a) the message

68

Table 5.3

Jobs	Average processing time (minutes)	Arrival rate (per minute)	Priority index
1	2	0.1	1
2	1	0.3	2
3	2.5	0.1	3

transmission time is constant; (b) the message transmission time is exponentially distributed; (c) the message transmission time is uniformly distributed. What are the corresponding mean response times for type 1 and type 4 messages ?

5. A message transmission system is responsible for transmitting two fixed length message types. The long messages are 50% longer than the short ones but twice as urgent. Supposing the system operates a non-preemptive priority rule, which message type should be given top priority?

6. An installation processes two types of jobs with the following characteristics. Type 1 has an arrival rate of 2/second; the mean and variance of its processing time are 100 ms and 2500 respectively. Type 2 has an arrival rate of 5/second; the mean and variance of its processing time are 40 ms and 625 respectively. The costs of keeping these 2 types of job in the system per second are £100 and £40 respectively. Determine the mean waiting cost incurred per second under optimal priority assignment. How does this compare with a situation in which the priorities are reversed?

7. A computer processes three types of jobs with characteristics given in Table 5.3. The system manager wishes to merge job classes 1 and 2 and assign top priority to the resultant class. Supposing both the relevant inter-arrival and processing times are all exponentially distributed, and that the system operates the preemptive resume priority rule, assess the advantages and disadvantages of such a merge.

8. A system manager plans to introduce priority scheduling into the installation. All jobs run in the installation have the same processing characteristics: mean processing time = 12 minutes, coefficient of variation = 0.75. The jobs are distinguishable into four priority classes, and the arrival pattern relating to each class is Poisson. Their hourly arrival rates (in ascending order of priority index) are 0.8, 0.7, 1.5 and 1. It is, however, considered unacceptable if the difference in mean response time between the highest priority and lowest priority jobs exceeds half an hour. Determine whether it is feasible to implement (a) a non-preemptive priority scheme, (b) a preemptive resume priority scheme.

9. In a batch processing system, a particular user is responsible for a program which has a known processing requirement of 2.5 hours. In a

questionnaire, the users are asked whether they would like the system to change from the current FIFO rule to the SJF rule. Suppose the job characteristics of the system are given as follows: arrival is Poisson with a rate of 0.5 jobs/hour; processing time is uniformly distributed with a mean of 1.5 hours. What should be the correct response of the user concerned? What is the mean turnaround time in each case?

10. For the $M/M/1$:SJF system, derive an expression for the mean response time of a job requiring a processing time of t units. What is the corresponding expression for the $M/M/1$ system?

11. A time-sharing system operates the RR rule with a small quantum size. Suppose job arrivals conform to a Poisson process and that the processor utilization is 70%. Assuming a mean processing time of 0.5 second, determine the extent of improvement/degradation of a LIFO system compared with this one if (a) the coefficient of variation of the processing time is 0.8, and (b) the coefficient of variation of the processing time is 1.5.

12. In a time-sharing system, suppose it is given that the processing requirement is geometrically distributed and that the percentage of jobs requiring exactly 1 quantum is 30%. Determine the percentage of jobs better off under the RR rule as compared with the FIFO rule.

13. The traffic intensity entering a time-sharing system operating the RR rule is 0.65. Suppose the quantum size is small and that arrivals conform to a Poisson process. Determine the normalized mean response time if (a) the swapping overhead is 10%, and (b) the swapping overhead is 20%.

14. Both the SJF and PS systems tend to discriminate in favour of short jobs and against long ones. For a job with a very small processing requirement, under which rule is it more favourably treated? For a job with a very large processing requirement, under which rule is it more favourably treated?

15. A system currently operates an RR rule with a quantum size $q = 1$ ms. It is observed that job arrivals conform to a Poisson pattern, and that jobs requiring exactly one quantum of service spend an average of 6 ms in the system. Suppose the processing requirement is geometrically distributed with an average requirement of two quanta. Estimate the mean response time for a job requiring 10 quanta under (a) the current RR system, and (b) the FIFO system.

CHAPTER 6

Systems with Practical Limitations

6.1 Introduction

In the previous chapter, we have been mainly concerned with the effect of scheduling. In the present chapter, we shall focus our attention on practical limitations imposed on the system by such factors as the size of the buffer and the number of jobs allowed to join the system. These systems are generally more complex to analyze than the corresponding ones without limitations as the additional restrictions have to been explicitly incorporated. Because of the relative complexity of these situations, most of the usable results are obtainable only in the case of exponentially distributed processing times. However, by confining attention to this simple distribution, we are able to extend the results to certain multi-server systems. The performance of all the systems discussed in this chapter essentially relies on one set of equations which govern the number of jobs in the system; by suitably adjusting the parameters in these equations, a wide variety of practical situations could be represented. These equations with general parameters will be developed in the next section; their applications to different processing situations will be examined in subsequent sections.

6.2 The Number of Jobs in the System

For the moment, we consider a system with arbitrary, unspecified, parameters; this is done for the sake of generality so that specific systems may be later represented by assigning suitable forms to these parameters. In particular, we shall focus our attention on the number of jobs in the system, which, for ease of reference, will be referred to as the *system state*. Here, we are mainly concerned with completely random transitions among system states where the probability of a transition occurring in a short time interval of duration h is proportional to h and is independent of what happens in other intervals. If the system is in state k ($k > 0$)—meaning that there are k jobs in the system—then we assume that in a short time interval of duration h, it can do one of the following:

(1) move to state $k - 1$ with probability $\mu_k h$ (this corresponds to a job departure);

70

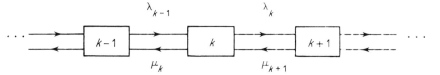

FIGURE 6.1.   State-transition-rate diagram

(2)   move to state $k + 1$ with probability $\lambda_k h$ (this corresponds to a job arrival);
(3)   remain in state k with probability $1 - \lambda_k h - \mu_k h$ (this corresponds to no change in the system).

Such movement is diagrammatically represented in Fig. 6.1, which is often called a *state-transition-rate diagram*. In such a situation, we wish to determine the state probabilities p_k, $k \geq 0$, of finding the system in state k. Here, we shall give a non-rigorous, intuitive derivation of the basic equations, called *balance equations*, which govern the state probabilities; a more rigorous derivation may be found in Kleinrock (1975).

Let us focus our attention on an arbitrary state $k > 0$, and consider the changes that take place in a short time interval of duration h; in particular, we shall compare the difference in probability Δp_k of finding the system in state k just before and just after the interval. Now, the probability of finding the system in state k increases if there is an arrival which causes the system to move to state k from state $(k - 1)$—this occurs with probability $p_{k-1}\lambda_{k-1}h$; likewise, this probability increases if there is a departure which causes the system to move to state k from state $(k + 1)$—this occurs with probability $p_{k+1}\mu_{k+1}h$. Thus, the increase in p_k is $(p_{k-1}\lambda_{k-1} + p_{k+1}\mu_{k+1})h$. On the other hand, the probability of finding the system in state k decreases if there is either an arrival or departure which causes the system to move from state k to a neighbouring state (i.e. either $k - 1$ or $k + 1$)—this decrease, analogous to that for the increase, is $(p_k\lambda_k + p_k\mu_k)h$. Therefore, the net change in probability of finding the system in state k at the expiration of the interval is

$$\Delta p_k = (p_{k-1}\lambda_{k-1} + p_{k+1}\mu_{k+1})h - (p_k\lambda_k + p_k\mu_k)h.$$

Now, suppose this change is positive; then as time goes on, the probability of finding the system in state k steadily increases, so that after a long time it eventually exceeds unity. This is of course not permitted, so that in order to obtain a meaningful equilibrium solution, we must insist that $\Delta p_k \leq 0$. On the other hand, if the change is negative, then eventually p_k moves to negative values, which again is not permitted. Thus, a meaningful equilibrium solution is possible only if $\Delta p_k = 0$. This implies that the increase and decrease must balance; i.e. $p_{k-1}\lambda_{k-1} + p_{k+1}\mu_{k+1} = p_k\lambda_k + p_k\mu_k$, $k > 0$. Applying the same argument to the boundary state 0, we likewise obtain $\lambda_0 p_0 = \mu_1 p_1$. Thus we have shown that, if a meaningful equilibrium solution exists, the state probabilities $\{p_k\}$ must obey the following set of balance equations:

$$p_{k-1}\lambda_{k-1} + p_{k+1}\mu_{k+1} = p_k\lambda_k + p_k\mu_k, \qquad k > 0,$$

$$\lambda_0 p_0 = \mu_1 p_1.$$

(6.2.1)

If we solve these equations successively, first expressing p_1 in terms of p_0, and then expressing p_2 in terms of p_1 and p_0, and so on, then we obtain

$$p_k = r_1 r_2 \cdots r_k p_0, \qquad k > 0,$$

where r_i signifies the arrival-to-departure rate ratio

$$r_i = \lambda_{i-1}/\mu_i.$$

If we denote the product $r_1 \cdots r_k$ by S_k, for $k > 0$, and define S_0 to be 1, then we have

$$p_k = p_0 S_k, \qquad k \geqslant 0.$$

(6.2.2)

Since the sum of all p_k, $k \geqslant 0$ must be 1, we obtain

$$p_0 = 1/\sum_{k=0}^{\infty} S_k.$$

(6.2.3)

Thus by virtue of (6.2.2) and (6.2.3), the state probabilities $\{p_k\}$ are completely determined. We note that this solution is meaningful only if $p_0 > 0$, since otherwise all the state probabilities are zero; physically, this means that the system must be occasionally empty. From (6.2.3), we see that this is true whenever

$$\sum_{k=0}^{\infty} S_k$$

is finite. In the rest of this chapter, we shall demonstrate how the above results could be applied to practical systems analysis; unless otherwise stated, the notations and assumptions of this section will be adopted. First of all, however, we shall apply it to the study of the M/M/1 queue; this will allow us to compare the results obtained from (6.2.2) and those obtained form the Pollaczek–Khintchine formula.

6.3 The System M/M/1

We recall that the state probability p_k signifies the probability of finding k jobs in the system. The model developed in the previous section can be used to represent the M/M/1 system by simply taking $\lambda_k = \lambda$ and $\mu_k = \mu$ for all relevant values of k. Thus, from (6.2.2), we have, on denoting λ/μ by ρ,

$$p_k = \rho^k p_0.$$

From (6.2.3), p_0 is given by $1 - \rho$, so that

$$p_k = (1 - \rho)\rho^k, \qquad k \geq 0,$$

which we recognize to be the geometric distribution. Its mean value $\bar{J}$ can be computed as in Example 2.2; the mean number of jobs $\bar{J}$ in the system is thus

$$\bar{J} = \rho/(1 - \rho),$$

which is in agreement with that obtained from the Pollaczek–Khintchine formula. From Little's formula, the mean response time $\bar{R}$ is

$$\bar{R} = 1/[\mu(1 - \rho)].$$

In fact, it can further be shown that (see Kleinrock (1975)) the cumulative distribution function $G(t)$ of the response time actually conforms to the exponential distribution:

$$G(t) = 1 - \exp[-\mu t(1 - \rho)], \qquad t \geq 0.$$

Example 6.1 A communications line operates at a speed of 9600 bps, and it is given that message arrivals form a Poisson stream with a rate of 250/minute and that their lengths are exponentially distributed with an average of 1000 bits. Supposing that the buffer size for storing outgoing messages is two, determine the fraction of overflow messages. Supposing, furthermore, it is required that 90% of the messages must be delivered within half a second, determine whether this can be achieved.

Solution. Here, the input rate is $250/60 = 4.17$ messages per second. The average transmission time is $1000/9600 = 0.1$ second, and the transmission rate is 9.6. This gives a value of $\rho = 0.43$. The probability that the buffer capacity is exceeded is

$$1 - p_0 - p_1 - p_2 = 1 - 0.57 - 0.25 - 0.11 = 7\%.$$

The fraction of messages which are delivered within half a second is $G(0.5) = 1 - \exp(-0.57 \times 9.6 \times 0.5) = 94\%$. Thus, the goal of having 90% of the messages delivered within 0.5 second is achievable. $\square$

6.4 The System M/M/1 With Limited Buffer

Here, we consider the allocation of buffer storage for accommodating data blocks for output by an I/O device. Fixed blocks of data are generated by an output process in which the times required to produce successive data blocks are exponentially distributed with mean $1/\lambda$. The data blocks produced are deposited in a buffer which can hold a maximum of M blocks. These blocks are then removed from the buffer for output by the device; we assume that this block consumption time is exponentially distributed with mean $1/\mu$. In this situation, overflows are not allowed, so that when the buffer is full, the data generation process would be suspended until a free buffer slot becomes available. Thus, we have

$$\lambda_k = \begin{cases} \lambda & 0 \leqslant k < M \\ 0 & k \geqslant M, \end{cases}$$

and $\mu_k = \mu$ for $k > 0$. Denoting λ/μ by ρ, we have therefore $S_k = \rho^k$ for $k \leqslant M$, and so from (6.2.2) we obtain the state probabilities

$$p_k = \begin{cases} \rho^k p_0 & 0 \leqslant k \leqslant M \\ 0 & k > M. \end{cases} \tag{6.4.1}$$

From (6.2.3), we find

$$p_0 = 1/\sum_{k=0}^{M} \rho^k = (1 - \rho)/(1 - \rho^{M+1}). \tag{6.4.2}$$

Thus we have

$$p_k = \rho^k(1 - \rho)/(1 - \rho^{M+1}), \qquad k = 0, 1, \ldots, M.$$

This is in fact a truncated geometric distribution (i.e. restricting the geometric distribution to a finite set of values); its mean value $\bar{J}(M)$ could be computed in much the same way as for the ordinary geometric distribution in Example 2.2 and equals

$$\rho/(1 - \rho) - (M + 1)\rho^{M+1}/(1 - \rho^{M+1}),$$

which represents the mean number of data blocks in the buffer. Accordingly, the average buffer storage utilization is $\bar{J}(M)/M$. The average data block generation rate in this situation would be less than λ because the generation activity is sometimes suspended to avoid overflow. In fact, the effective generation rate is λ times the fraction of time that the data generation process is in operation or $\lambda(1 - p_M)$. It is interesting to note from (6.2.3) that here $p_0 > 0$ for all values of ρ, since we are dealing with a finite sum. The following example further amplifies this point.

Example 6.2 Suppose a buffer can accommodate a maximum of 24 data blocks and that the mean block consumption time $1/\mu$ is the same as the mean data generation time $1/\lambda$. Calculate (a) the buffer storage utilization, and (b) the reduction in data generation rate due to buffer restriction. What is the reduction in data generation rate if the buffer can accommodate only nine blocks?

Solution. Here $\lambda = \mu$ and so $\rho = 1$. From (6.4.1), this implies that $p_k =$ constant for $k = 0, 1 \ldots, M$; since Σp_k over this set of values must be one, we thus obtain $p_k = 1/(M + 1)$ for $0 \leqslant k \leqslant M$. The average number of blocks $\bar{J}(M)$ in the buffer is $(0 + 1 + \cdots + M)/(M + 1) = M/2$, which gives a buffer utilization of 50%. The effective data generation rate for $M = 24$ is

$\lambda(1 - \frac{1}{25})$ or $24\lambda/25$, which is a reduction of 4%. Similarly, for $M = 9$, the effective data generation rate is $9\lambda/10$, which is a reduction of 10%. $\square$

6.5 The System M/M/1 with Finite Population: The Interactive Response Time Formula

Here, we consider an interactive system supporting M active user terminals. We suppose that the time that each user requires to generate an input request to the processor, often called the *think time*, is exponentially distributed with mean $1/\lambda$, and that the time required by the processor to service a request is exponentially distributed with mean $1/\mu$. At any one time, we suppose that each user is allowed at most one outstanding request; if a user terminal is awaiting results to be returned from processing after a submission, we say that it is in a wait state. If the processor is idle, then all M terminals are eligible to submit requests for processing, so that the aggregate rate of submission in such a situation is $M\lambda$. At the other extreme, if all M users are in a wait state, then no more submission can take place and the submission rate is zero. Thus, we have a submission rate which is dependent on the number of terminals in the wait state, which we shall take to be the system state for this queue; i.e.

$$\lambda_k = \begin{cases} (M - k)\lambda & 0 \leqslant k < M \\ 0 & k \geqslant M, \end{cases}$$

and $\mu_k = \mu$ for $k > 0$. Substituting these parameters into (6.2.2) and denoting the ratio μ/λ by r, we obtain

$$p_k = \begin{cases} r^{-k} p_0 M!/(M - k)! & 0 \leqslant k \leqslant M \\ 0 & k > M, \end{cases} \tag{6.5.1}$$

where from (6.2.3)

$$p_0 = 1/[\sum_{k=0}^{M} r^{-k} M!/(M - k)!]. \tag{6.5.2}$$

Substituting (6.5.2) into (6.5.1) and multiplying both the numerator and denominator of the result by the factor r^M and suitably changing the index of summation in the denominator, we obtain

$$p_k = [r^{M-k}/(m - k)!][\sum_{j=0}^{M} r^j/j!], \qquad 0 \leqslant k \leqslant M. \tag{6.5.3}$$

In particular, for $k = 0$, we have

$$p_0 = [r^M/M!]/[\sum_{j=0}^{M} r^j/j!].$$ (6.5.4)

This ratio, which we shall denote by $q(r|M)$, occurs quite frequently in queueing theory and is widely graphed and tabulated; its use will be illustrated in Example 6.3. The fraction of time that the processor is busy gives the processor utilization ρ; i.e. $\rho = 1 - p_0$. We note that, unlike in cases where the population is infinite, the utilization here is different from λ/μ because the input does not enter the system at a steady rate but is dependent on the number of terminals in the wait state.

Next, we turn our attention to the response time as experienced by the individual user. We shall first focus our attention on the mean inter-submission time $\bar{T}$ relating to a given terminal. This time $\bar{T}$ is made up of two components: the mean think time $(1/\lambda)$ and the mean response time $\bar{R}$ during which the terminal is in the wait state; i.e. $\bar{T} = \bar{R} + 1/\lambda$. The average request submission rate of a given terminal is $1/\bar{T}$, and so the overall average submission rate as seen by the processor is $M/\bar{T}$. Since each submission requires an average processing time of $1/\mu$ seconds, the processor utilization can also be obtained by multiplying this by the overall submission rate, which gives $M/(\mu\bar{T})$. Equating this to ρ, we can then solve for the unknown $\bar{R}$; i.e.

$$\rho = M/(\mu\bar{T}) = M/[\mu(\bar{R} + 1/\lambda)];$$ (6.5.5)

this yields

$$\bar{R} = M/(\mu\rho) - 1/\lambda,$$ (6.5.6)

which is often referred to as the *interactive response time formula*. The normalized mean response time $\bar{R}^*$ is $\bar{R}$ divided by the mean processing time $1/\mu$:

$$\bar{R}^* = M/\rho - r.$$ (6.5.7)

For large M, the processor is heavily utilized so that $\rho \simeq 1$ and so $\bar{R}^* \simeq M - r$. From (6.5.5), the overall mean submission rate $M/\bar{T}$ can be written as $\mu\rho$, so that applying Little's formula to (6.5.6), we can calculate the mean number of terminals $\bar{J}$ in the wait state:

$$\bar{J} = \mu\rho\bar{R} = M - \rho r,$$ (6.5.8)

which for large M would likewise be $\bar{J} \simeq M - r$. Note that in deriving (6.5.7) and (6.5.8), no specific assumption was made concerning the think time and processing time distributions; therefore these mean value formulae are valid for arbitrarily distributed think time and processing time for a given level of processor utilization.

Example 6.3 Consider an interactive system with 30 active terminals. The user think time and processor service time are both exponentially distributed;

the former has a mean of 20 seconds, and the latter has a mean of 1 second. Determine (a) the processor utilization; (b) the normalized mean request response time; (c) the mean number of terminals in the wait state.

Solution. Here $M = 30$, $1/\lambda = 20$, $1/\mu = 1$, so that $r = \mu/\lambda = 20$. This implies $p_0 = q(20|30)$, and $\rho = 1 - p_0$. From tabulated values, it is found that $q(20|30)$ is approximately 0.007. Thus, the normalized mean response time, from (6.5.7), is $30/0.993 - 20 = 10.2$ seconds, and the mean number of terminals in the wait state, from (6.5.8), is $30 - 20 \times 0.993 = 10.1$. $\square$

6.6   The M/M/m Loss System: Erlang's B Formula

Here, we consider a multi-processor system where there is no waiting room so that jobs which arrive when all processors are busy have to leave without receiving any service. If m denotes the number of processors, this arrival behaviour may be represented as

$$\lambda_k = \begin{cases} \lambda & 0 \leqslant k < m \\ 0 & k \geqslant m. \end{cases}$$

Because there are multiple processors, the service rate of the system steps up in accordance with the number of jobs in the system; these jobs are necessarily receiving service. Thus $\mu_k = k\mu$ for $0 \leqslant k \leqslant m$. From (6.2.2) and (6.2.3) and denoting λ/μ by ρ, we obtain

$$p_k = [\rho^k/k!]/[\sum_{j=0}^{m} \rho^j/j!], \qquad 0 \leqslant k \leqslant m. \qquad (6.6.1)$$

In particular, p_m signifies the probability of a full system under which condition any arriving job is lost; the corresponding expression obtained by setting $k = m$ in (6.6.1) is commonly referred to as Erlang's B formula which gives the proportion of jobs lost to the system. From (6.5.4), we see that p_m may be expressed as the ratio $q(\rho|m)$ defined there, and so from standard tables this probability can be obtained in a straightforward manner.

Example 6.4   Consider a data communications system with dial-up connection making use of three lines. Supposing λ and μ here are the same, determine, using the model in this section, the percentage of lost calls.

Solution.   Here $\rho = 1$, so that the percentage of lost calls is simply $q(1|3)$ which, from tabulated values, is approximately equal to 6%. $\square$

6.7   The System M/M/m: Erlang's C Formula

We consider again a multi-processor system here similar to the one in the previous section, except that we now have unlimited buffer to accommodate arriving jobs. In this situation, we have $\lambda_k = \lambda$, $k \geq 0$. Like the previous section, the service rate of the system initially increases as more jobs enter the system, but when all the m processors are busy, the system reaches its maximum service rate; i.e.

$$\mu_k = \begin{cases} k\mu & 0 \leq k < m \\ m\mu & k \geq m. \end{cases}$$

From Chapter 3, the condition of a stable system is $\lambda/(m\mu) < 1$; the quantity $\lambda/(m\mu)$ represents the utilization of an individual processor, and we shall denote it by ρ here. From (6.2.2), we obtain

$$p_k = \begin{cases} (m\rho)^k p_0/k! & 0 \leq k \leq m \\ m^m \rho^k p_0/m! & k > m, \end{cases} \tag{6.7.1}$$

where

$$p_0 = 1/\{[\sum_{k=0}^{m-1} (m\rho)^k/k!] + (mp)^m/[m!(1 - \rho)]\}. \tag{6.7.2}$$

The number of busy processors equals to the number of jobs in the system when these are less than m, and equals m when there are m or more jobs in the system. It can be verified that this is equal to

$$\sum_{k=1}^{m} kp_k + \sum_{k>m} mp_k = m\rho. \tag{6.7.3}$$

The probability that an arrival has to queue, rather receiving service immediately, is frequently of interest. The corresponding expression is called Erlang's C formula; this signifies a situation when all m processors are busy and is given by

$$\sum_{k=m}^{\infty} p_k.$$

In making use of the ratio $q(m\rho|m)$ defined by (6.5.4), it can be verified that this may be written as

$$q(m\rho|m)/\{1 - \rho[1 - q(m\rho|m)]\}. \tag{6.7.4}$$

From tabulated values, this can be obtained in a straightforward manner.

The mean number of jobs $\bar{Q}$ in the queue (excluding those being processed) is

$$\sum_{k>m} (k - m)p_k = \sum_{k>m} (k - m)m^m \rho^k p_0/m!,$$

which can be evaluated in much the same way as in the case of the geometric distribution (see Section 2.3); this is found to be

$$\bar{Q} = (m\rho)^m \lambda \mu p_0/[(m - 1)! (m\mu - \lambda)^2]. \tag{6.7.5}$$

If we again make use of the ratio $q(mp|m)$, it can be verified that p_0 may be written as

$$p_0 = m!/\{(mp)^m[1/q(mp|m) + p/(1 - p)]\},$$

so that $\bar{Q}$ may be obtained from tabulated values. The mean waiting time $\bar{W}$, mean response time $\bar{R}$, and mean number of jobs in the system $\bar{J}$ can be obtained by application of Little's formulae.

6.8 The System M/M/∞

The results of the loss system considered in Section 6.6 could be extended in a straightforward manner to deal with the case where the number of processors is very large or infinite; in this case, of course, no job is lost to the system as there is always a processor available for every job. Letting $m \to \infty$ in (6.6.1), we recognize that the state probability is simply given by the Poisson distribution; i.e.

$$p_k = \exp(-p)p^k/k! \qquad k \geqslant 0. \qquad (6.8.1)$$

The mean number of jobs in the system, which is the same as the number of processors in use, is simply $p = \lambda/\mu$. In fact, it can be shown (see Gross and Harris (1974)) that the same Poisson state probabilities given by (6.8.1) also holds for the system M/G/∞ with arbitrary service distribution. The response time of this system is, of course, the same as the service time.

Example 6.5 Consider an M/G/∞ system in which the job arrival rate is 50% higher than the service rate. Determine (a) the mean number of jobs in the system, and (b) the probability that the number of jobs in the system is higher than the mean value.

Solution. Here $p = 1.5$, so that the mean number of jobs in the system is 1.5. The probability that the number of jobs in the system is two or more is $1 - \exp(-1.5) - 1.5 \exp(-1.5) = 0.44$. □

6.9 Summary

In this chapter, we have looked at systems where the change in the number of jobs occurs completely randomly over time. At any small time interval, the magnitude of change can involve only at most one job, and the likelihood of a change taking place is dependent on the number of jobs present. By suitably adjusting this dependency relationship, we are able to model the M/M/1 system with limited and unlimited buffer. Here, we are able to obtain explicitly the distribution of the number of jobs in the system. We have also introduced the interactive response time formula for studying interactive systems performance using the M/M/1 system with finite population. The multiserver system M/M/m has been studied under two settings: zero buffer, and infinite buffer. These models lead to the well-known Erlang's B and Erlang's C formulae respectively; they both give the probability that all the servers are found to be busy on the arrival of a job. Finally, results are presented for the distribution of the number of jobs in the system for the queues M/M/∞ and M/G/∞; they are both seen to conform to the Poisson distribution.

6.10   Exercises

1.   A communications line operates at a speed of 9600 bps, and it is given that message arrivals form a Poisson stream with rate 600/minute and that their lengths are exponentially distributed with an average of 500 bits. Supposing that the buffer size for storing outgoing messages is limited, and that the fraction of overflow messages is not allowed to exceed 5%, determine the minimum amount of buffer that must be allocated to this system.

2.   For a given communications line, it is given that message arrivals form a Poisson stream with rate 300/minute, and that their lengths are exponentially distributed with an average of 1500 bits. Supposing it is required that 90% of the messages must be delivered within half a second, determine the minimum line speed to make this possible.

3.   Suppose a buffer can accommodate a maximum of 20 data blocks, and it is given that the ratio of the mean block consumption time $1/\mu$ to the mean data generation time $1/\lambda$ is $\frac{3}{4}$. Calculate (a) the buffer storage utilization, and (b) the reduction in data generation rate due to buffer restriction. You should state clearly any assumptions that you make in obtaining the results.

4.   Consider an interactive system with 60 active terminals. The user think time and processor service time are both exponentially distributed; the former has a mean of 25 seconds, and the latter has a mean of 0.5 second. Suppose it is given that $q(50|60) = 0.02$. Show that the normalized mean response time is approximately 11 seconds.

5.   It is given that the mean number of busy processors in an M/M/5 multiprocessor system is 4, and that the arrival rate is 3 jobs per second. Determine the service rate of an individual processor.

6.   Consider an M/M/∞ system in which the job arrival rate is 75% higher than the service rate. Determine (a) the mean number of jobs in the system, and (b) the probability that the number of jobs in the system is between two and six.

CHAPTER 7

Networks of Queues

7.1 Introduction

In the previous chapters, we have been concerned only with isolated queues, and no attempt has been made to go beyond the arrival and departure mechanisms other than imposing a prescribed structure on them. In practical situations, queues are often interconnected to form networks, and it is by considering the entire interacting network of queues that meaningful performance information on the system can be derived. A queueing network consists of a number of service nodes, each of which may, in turn, consist of one or more servers; these nodes are connected by directed arcs which represent the flow of traffic through the system. A job flowing through the network typically consists of several requests requiring service from the constituent nodes. A typical queueing network is shown in Fig. 7.1, where external traffic can enter the network via either node 1 or node 3; jobs entering via node 1 can follow route 1–2 or route 1–3–4–2 before departing from the network; likewise, jobs entering via node 3 can follow the route 3–4–2 before departing from the network. Very often each arc has a probability associated with it signifying the likelihood of a job following it; typically this probability is assumed to depend only on the source and destination nodes, irrespective of the detailed route of the job.

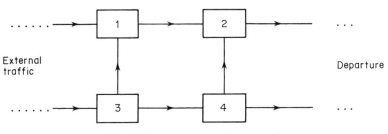

FIGURE 7.1.   A queueing network

Depending on whether external arrivals and departures are allowed, a queueing network may be classified as open or closed. An *open queueing network* is one in which there are arrivals from, and departures to, the outside;

82

while in a *closed queueing network*, there are neither external arrivals nor departures, and a fixed number of jobs are trapped inside the network circulating among the different nodes. An open queueing network is called *feedforward* if no jobs are allowed to visit the same node twice. Our discussions in the previous chapters have been mainly confined to a special case of an open network consisting of a single node.

In order to meaningfully analyze a queueing network, one has to examine the interaction among service nodes. As we saw in Fig. 7.1, the departures from one node often form the input into another node. Discovering the pattern of departures from a service node—often called the *output process*—is therefore crucial to the assessment of queueing network performance. The output from a service node is obviously dependent on the service distribution, but it must be noted that the inter-departure distribution is in general different from the service distribution because when there is an intervening idle period, the interval between successful departures is longer than the service time. The output of a service node are, of course, point events which admit both a point description and an interval description. They are in general very complicated; however, in the case of an exponential node—i.e. one in which the service times are exponentially distributed—the output does exhibit a remarkable simplicity. This forms the subject of the next section.

7.2   The Output of an M/M/m Queue: Burke's Theorem

Here, we consider the departure point events from the M/M/m system with arrival and service rates equal to λ and μ respectively. The server utilization ρ, as we saw in Chapter 3, is given by $\lambda/(m\mu)$. We shall focus our attention on the mean number of departures in a small time interval of duration h. If the system is in state one—meaning that there exists a single job in the system and, necessarily, it is in service—then because of the exponential characteristics of the service time, the rate of departure is μ so that the mean number of departure under this condition is μh. Likewise if the system state is k $(1 < k \leq m)$, the mean number of departures is $k\mu h$; if the system state is greater than m, then since there is only a total of m servers the mean number of departure is $m\mu h$. Denoting the state probabilities by $\{p_k\}$ and averaging over the different probabilities, we obtain for the mean number of departures in a small time interval of duration h:

$$\mu h \{ \sum_{k=1}^{m} k p_k + \sum_{k>m} m p_k \}.$$

From (6.7.3), we find that this equals $m\mu\rho h$, and from the definition of ρ, this is λh. Furthermore, because of the exponential character of the service distribution, the events in different intervals are independent; we therefore conclude that the output is a Poisson process with rate λ. This result is quite remarkable and introduces substantial simplification to the analysis of certain

FIGURE 7.2.　A two-node tandem network

types of exponential queueing networks. It essentially says that, from the viewpoint of an observer positioned at the exit of the service node, the node is transparent and the input traffic behaves as if it had bypassed the service node completely; this simple result is known as Burke's theorem. Intuitively, one would expect the mean input rate and mean output rate to be more or less the same anyway because all jobs would obtain service eventually and flow through the node; Burke's theorem, however, asserts something stronger: the input and output distributions are actually the same. The next section assesses the impact of Burke's theorem on queueing network analysis.

7.3　Feedforward Networks

The consequence of Burke's theorem, coupled with the fact that the completely random nature of Poisson streams is preserved in merging and splitting operations (see Chapter 2) imply that the input to each node in a feedforward exponential queueing network is necessarily Poisson. This means that each node, when considered in isolation, can be analyzed as a separate $M/M/m$ node. But what about the analysis of the entire network as a whole? Although in general it is true that the number of jobs in different nodes are independent (see Gelenbe and Mitrani (1980) for a proof), it is, however, not true that the corresponding waiting times (excluding service) are independent. This can be seen by considering the two-node tandem network in Fig. 7.2. Supposing a job experiences a long waiting time in node 1, then this may be caused by having a large number of jobs ahead of it; and these same jobs would likewise cause substantial delay to the job in question in node 2. Thus a long delay at node 1 may mean a long delay at node 2 as well. In spite of such dependence, the mean delay, like the mean number of jobs, for the entire network nevertheless may be found by combining those at individual nodes, since the additivity of the mean is also valid for dependent quantities. It is worth pointing out that the terminal nodes of a feedforward network—these are nodes where the output from them are not fed into any other nodes—are allowed to have general service distribution without destroying the tractability of the network, since these outputs represent departures from the network and so the corresponding distribution is not of interest from the viewpoint of response time analysis.

Example 7.1 Similar messages from two remote locations are entered via communications lines for processing and storage. Because of the differing line

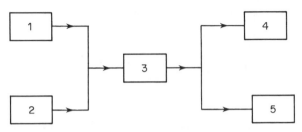

FIGURE 7.3. Network of Example 7.1

speeds, the respective service rates of these lines are different and equal to μ_1 and μ_2; the corresponding message input rates are λ_1, and λ_2, and both inputs are given to be Poisson. The messages are then processed by the CPU with service rate μ_3 before outputting to one of two storage devices with service rates μ_4 and μ_5 respectively, each of which is chosen with the same probability. Supposing the line service times, the CPU processing time, and the service time of the storage device having service rate μ_4 are all exponentially distributed, and the service time of the remaining storage device is constant, determine the average elapsed time for an arbitrary message to flow through such a system.

Solution.   This network may be represented diagrammatically as in Fig. 7.3, where each node is identified by the subscript of its service rate. From the Pollaczek–Khintchine formula, the mean response times at node 1 and node 2 are respectively

$$\bar{R}_1 = 1/(\mu_1 - \lambda_1)$$
$$\bar{R}_2 = 1/(\mu_2 - \lambda_2).$$

The combined output from nodes 1 and 2, from Burke's theorem, is Poisson with rate $\lambda_1 + \lambda_2$, and so the mean response time at node 3 is

$$\bar{R}_3 = 1/[\mu_3 - (\lambda_1 + \lambda_2)].$$

The inputs to either node 4 or node 5 are Poisson with rate $0.5(\lambda_1 + \lambda_2)$. The mean response time at node 4 is

$$\bar{R}_4 = 1/[\mu_4 - 0.5(\lambda_1 + \lambda_2)].$$

Likewise, the mean response time at node 5 is, from the Pollaczek–Khintchine formula

$$\bar{R}_5 = \{1/[4\mu_5/(\lambda_1 + \lambda_2) - 2] + 1\}/\mu_5$$

Hence the mean response time for messages entering at node 1 is

$$\bar{R}' = \bar{R}_1 + \bar{R}_3 + 0.5(\bar{R}_4 + \bar{R}_5),$$

and that for messages entering at node 2 is

$$\bar{R}'' = \bar{R}_2 + \bar{R}_3 + 0.5(\bar{R}_4 + \bar{R}_5).$$

Since the proportion of messages entering of node i ($i = 1, 2$) is

$$\lambda_i/(\lambda_1 + \lambda_2),$$

the required average elapsed time for an arbitrary message is therefore

$$(\lambda_1\bar{R}' + \lambda_2\bar{R}'')/(\lambda_1 + \lambda_2). \quad \square$$

Example 7.2 Consider a tandem queueing network consisting of N single server exponential nodes with respective rates $\mu_1, \ldots, \mu_N$. Calculate the total average response of the network if the input is Poisson with rate λ. What is the average number of jobs in the network?

Solution. By Burke's theorem, the input to a typical node k is Poisson with rate λ, so that the associated mean response time is

$$1/(\mu_k - \lambda),$$

and by Little's formula, the associated mean number of jobs is

$$\lambda/(\mu_k - \lambda).$$

The total average response time is

$$\sum_{k=1}^{N} 1/(\mu_k - \lambda),$$

and the total average number of jobs in the system is

$$\sum_{k=1}^{N} \lambda/(\mu_k - \lambda). \quad \triangledown$$

7.4 General Exponential Open Queueing Network: Jackson's Theorem

By virtue of Burke's theorem and the fact that the merging and splitting of Poisson streams remain Poisson, one might think that for a network with feedback (i.e. one in which jobs are allowed to visit the same node twice or more) the input to each node should also be Poisson. This unfortunately is not true, because feedback would introduce into the input stream some dependence on the past and so gives rise to a non-Poisson input stream.

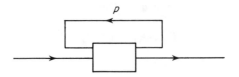

FIGURE 7.4. A simple feedback network

Consider, for example, the simple feedback queue in Fig. 7.4, where in addition to normal external arrivals and departures, a given proportion of jobs are recycled back for processing by the server: each job after completing service is assumed to immediately return to join the end of the queue with a fixed probability p. Suppose the mean service time is short and the recycle probability p is high. In such a situation, if it is given that a large number of arrivals has occurred in the recent past, then the present rate of arrivals is likely to be high because a large number of requests is recycled back. This indicates that the arrival behaviour is no longer memoryless and so would not be Poisson.

In spite of the complication introduced by the non-Poisson nature of nodal input in a general network with feedback, it is nevertheless shown in Jackson (1963) that each node does *behave* as if it were subject to Poisson input. This remarkable simplification is often known as Jackson's theorem; a proof of this theorem may be found, for example, in Gelenbe and Mitrani (1980).

Jackson's theorem **Consider a general N-node open network in which the ith node is a M/M/m_i queue with external arrival rate λ_i. Having completed service at node i, a job either proceeds to node $j\,(1 \leqslant j \leqslant N)$ with probability q_{ij} or departs from the network with probability**

$$1 - \sum_{j=1}^{N} q_{ij}.$$

Then, in such a situation, each node behaves as if it were an independent node with Poisson input as concerns the number of jobs in it; the total input rate $I_i\,(i = 1, 2, \ldots, N)$ to the ith node is the sum of the arrival rates both from within the network and from outside and is given by

$$I_i = \lambda_i + \sum_{j=1}^{N} q_{ji}I_j. \tag{7.4.1}$$

As we have noted in the previous section, the waiting times at different nodes of a feedforward network are in general not independent; this lack of independence obviously also applies to a more general queueing network with

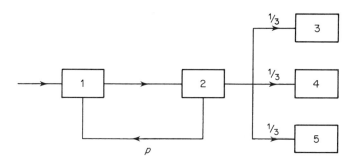

FIGURE 7.5. Network of Example 7.3

feedback allowed. By virtue of Jackson's theorem, it is possible, as in the case of feedforward networks, to obtain the mean delays and mean number of jobs present for the entire network by simply combining those obtained from the analysis of individual nodes. In order to obtain the mean delay at a given node, one must first solve for its total input rate from the system of equations (7.4.1), which are often known as the *traffic equations*; the solution of course is dependent on the probabilities q_{ij}, which are called the *routing frequencies*.

Example 7.3 Consider a message switching centre receiving messages sent to it via a given communications line. The message transmission time on this line is exponentially distributed with mean $1/\mu_1$. When a message is received, it is checked for errors at the switching centre; the checking time is exponentially distributed with mean $1/\mu_2$. If an error is found, then the message is re-transmitted from the source. From past experience, it is found that a pro-portion p of the messages are in error and consequently have to be re-transmitted. If a message is found to be error-free, then it will be routed to one of three destinations, each being chosen with equal probability. These three destinations are connected to the switching centre by three separate communications lines with different speeds. The transmission times of these outgoing messages are exponentially distributed with respective means $1/\mu_3$, $1/\mu_4$, $1/\mu_5$. Given that the source message traffic is Poisson with rate λ, determine the average total delay experienced by a typical message in flowing through the network. What is the average total number of messages awaiting outgoing transmission (including those being transmitted) from the switching centre?

Solution. This network may be represented diagrammatically as in Fig. 7.5, where each node is identified by the subscript of its service rate. We first determine the input into each node using the traffic equations (7.4.1). These equations are:

$$I_1 = \lambda + pI_2$$
$$I_2 = I_1$$
$$I_3 = I_2/3$$
$$I_4 = I_2/3$$
$$I_5 = I_2/3$$

That is,

$$I_1 = I_2 = \lambda/(1 - p)$$
$$I_3 = I_4 = I_5 = \lambda/[3(1 - p)].$$

From these, we can calculate the response time at each node using the Pollaczek–Khintchine formula

$$\bar{R}_1 = 1/\{\mu_1 - \lambda/(1 - p)\}$$
$$\bar{R}_2 = 1/\{\mu_2 - \lambda/(1 - p)\}$$
$$\bar{R}_3 = 1/\{\mu_3 - \lambda/[3(1 - p)]\}$$
$$\bar{R}_4 = 1/\{\mu_4 - \lambda/[3(1 - p)]\}$$
$$\bar{R}_5 = 1/\{\mu_5 - \lambda/[3(1 - p)]\}.$$

For a given source message, the probability that is has to go through nodes 1 and 2 exactly $(n + 1)$ times means that it was transmitted in error for exactly n times and transmitted error-free once—this happens with probability $p^n(1 - p)$. Thus the number of times that a message has to join the switching centre queue is geometrically distributed; its mean is $1/(1 - p)$. Thus the mean total delay flowing through nodes 1 and 2 is $(\bar{R}_1 + \bar{R}_2)/(1 - p)$. Since from node 2 it can proceed to nodes 3, 4 or 5 with probability $\frac{1}{3}$, the remaining average delay on leaving node 2 is thus $(\bar{R}_3 + \bar{R}_4 + \bar{R}_5)/3$. Thus the mean total delay in flowing through the entire network is

$$(\bar{R}_1 + \bar{R}_2)/(1 - p) + (\bar{R}_3 + \bar{R}_4 + \bar{R}_5)/3.$$

Next, the mean number of messages $\bar{J}_i$ at node i is by Little's formula $\bar{J}_i = I_i\bar{R}_i$. Thus the mean total number of messages in nodes 3, 4 and 5 is

$$\bar{J}_3 + \bar{J}_4 + \bar{J}_5 = \{\lambda/[3(1 - p)]\}(\bar{R}_3 + \bar{R}_4 + \bar{R}_5). \quad \square$$

Example 7.4 Consider the queueing network in Fig. 7.6 consisting of two single server exponential service nodes both having the same service rate. Upon leaving node 2, a job proceeds either to node 1 with probability q, or rejoins node 2 with probability p, or departs from the network with probability r, where $p + q + r = 1$. External arrivals into the network follow a Poisson process and they always come through node 1. Supposing it is found that the

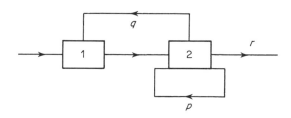

FIGURE 7.6.   Network of Example 7.4

utilization level of node 1 relative to that of node 2 is 75%, determine the probability p that a job immediately rejoins node 2 upon leaving it. If the utilization of node 2 is 60%, what is the probability that both nodes have the same number of jobs?

Solution.   Denoting the external input rate by λ, we first solve for the input rates for each node using the traffic equations (7.4.1),

$$I_1 = \lambda + qI_2$$
$$I_2 = I_1 + pI_2.$$

This gives

$$I_1 = \lambda(r + q)/r$$
$$I_2 = \lambda/r.$$

Since the service rates at both nodes are the same, the ratio of their utilization is simply given by that of the input rates:

$$I_1/I_2 = r + q,$$

which is given to be $\tfrac{3}{4}$; since $p + q + r = 1$, it therefore follows that $p = 25\%$.

Next, we denote the utilizations of nodes 1 and 2 by ρ_1 and ρ_2 respectively. The probability that node 1 has k jobs in it is, from the previous chapter,

$$\rho_1^k (1 - \rho_1).$$

Likewise the probability that node 2 has k jobs in it is

$$\rho_2^k (1 - \rho_2).$$

From Jackson's theorem, the number of jobs in these nodes are independent, so that the probability that both nodes have k jobs in them is the product

$$\rho_1^k (1 - \rho_1)\, \rho_2^k (1 - \rho_2).$$

Summing this over all $k \geq 0$, we obtain the required probability

$$\{(1 - \rho_1)(1 - \rho_2)\}/\{1 - \rho_1\rho_2\}$$
$$= \{(1 - 0.45)(1 - 0.6)\}/\{1 - (0.6)(0.45)\}$$
$$= 0.22/0.73 = 30.1\% \quad \square$$

7.5 Closed Queueing Networks

While the analysis of an open queueing network with exponential nodes is relatively straightforward and certainly manageable, the same cannot be said for a closed queueing network. Since the number of jobs within the network is fixed with no external arrivals or departures, the states of different nodes are necessarily dependent, because if all jobs are, for instance, enqueued to a given node, other nodes are empty. Unlike for an open network, no neat closed-form solution generally exists for a closed queueing network. For a closed queueing network consisting of N single server exponential nodes with service rates μ_i, $1 \leq i \leq N$, a fixed number of jobs K, and routing frequencies q_{ij}, the performance of the network is crucially dependent on the quantities

$$G(k) = \sum \prod_{i=1}^{N} \rho_i^{n_i}, \qquad k = 1, 2, \ldots, K, \qquad (7.5.1)$$

where the summation is taken over all non-negative integers $n_1, n_2, \ldots, n_N$ such that $n_1 + n_2 + \cdots + n_N = k$, and $\rho_i = I_i/\mu_i$, $\{I_i\}$ being a solution to the equations

$$I_j = \sum_{i=1}^{N} I_i q_{ij} \qquad (7.5.2)$$

From $\{G(k)\}$, the mean number of jobs $\bar{J}_i$ at node i may be determined from

$$\bar{J}_i = \sum_{j=1}^{K} \rho_i^j G(K - j)/G(K), \qquad (7.5.3)$$

where $G(0)$ is defined to be 1, and the throughput at node i is given by

$$\lambda_i = I_i G(K - 1)/G(K). \qquad (7.5.4)$$

The mean response time $\bar{R}_i$ at node i can thus be obtained from Little's formula; i.e.

$$\bar{R}_i = \bar{J}_i/\lambda_i. \qquad (7.5.5)$$

The computation of the sequence $G(k)$, $1 \leq k \leq N$ is in general non-trivial, and requires a total of approximately NK multiplications and additions. Similar results also exist for multi-server nodes with the associated computation accordingly more involved. A detailed derivation of the above results and their extensions may be found in Gelenbe and Mitrani (1980). An illustration of the above method is given in the following example.

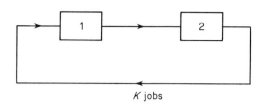

K jobs

FIGURE 7.7.   Network of Example 7.5

Example 7.5   Consider a two-node cyclic network with K jobs as shown in Fig. 7.7, where the service times at both nodes are assumed to be exponentially distributed with a common service rate μ. We shall determine the performance of this system using the above method. Since the routing frequencies equal 1, we have from equation (7.5.2) $I_1 = I_2$; denoting this common value by I, we have $\rho = I/\mu$ for both nodes. Substituting this into (7.5.1), we obtain

$$G(k) = \sum \rho^k.$$

The number of terms in this sum can be seen as follows. If $n_1 = i$, then n_2 is automatically determined and equals $k - i$. Thus by varying n_1 from 0 to k, all possibilities are exhausted; this means that the number of terms in the sum is $(k + 1)$; i.e.

$$G(k) = (k + 1)\,\rho^k.$$

From (7.5.3) the mean number of jobs in node i is

$$\bar{J}_i = \sum_{j=1}^{K} \rho^j(K + 1 - j)\rho^{K-j}/[(K + 1)\rho^K]$$

$$= \sum_{j=1}^{K} (K + 1 - j)/(K + 1) = K/2.$$

We notice that this is independent of i; this result is not at all surprising because the two nodes are identical and really indistinguishable in the network. Similarly, if the number of nodes is increased to N, the mean number of jobs in each node, by symmetry, is K/N.   □

In the next chapter, closed queueing networks will be further discussed from the standpoint of operational analysis.

7.6   Summary

In this chapter, we have examined the behaviour of queueing networks which consist of a collection of interacting service nodes. In an open network there are external arrivals and departures. In a closed network, on the other hand,

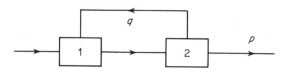

FIGURE 7.8. Network of Exercise 2

no external arrivals and departures are allowed, and a fixed number of jobs are trapped inside the network. For an open queueing network where the external arrivals conform to a Poisson process, and where all service nodes have exponential service distributions, then a remarkable simplification due to Jackson's theorem is possible: the mean delay and the mean number of jobs at each node can be analyzed as if it were an isolated M/M/m node. For a closed queueing network, no such simplification is possible; its performance can only be determined computationally with no closed-form expression available.

7.7 Exercises

1. Consider a tandem queueing network consisting of N single server exponential nodes with respective rates $\mu_1, \ldots, \mu_N$. Derive an expression for the maximum throughput for this network.

2. Consider the network given in Fig. 7.8, where $p + q = 1$. Write down the traffic equations for this network, and hence derive an expression for the average response time for each node.

3. For the network in the previous exercise, derive an expression for the average time taken for a job to flow through the network. Hence determine a value for p which minimizes this average flow time.

4. Similar messages from two remote locations are entered via communications lines for processing and storage. Because of the differing line speeds, the respective service rates of these lines are different and equal to $\mu_1 = 5$ messages per second and $\mu_2 = 6$ messages per second; the corresponding message input rates are $\lambda_1 = 1$ and $\lambda_2 = 2$, and both inputs are given to be Poisson. The messages are then processed by the CPU with service rate $\mu = 12$. Supposing the line service times and the CPU processing time are exponentially distributed, determine the average elapsed time for an arbitrary message to flow through such a system.

5. Consider a message switching centre receiving messages sent to it via a given communications line. The message transmission time on this line is exponentially distributed with mean $1/\mu_1$. When a message is received, it is checked for errors at the switching centre; the checking time is exponentially distributed with mean $1/\mu_2$. If an error is found, then the message is retransmitted from the source. It is found that a proportion p of the messages are in error and consequently have to be re-transmitted. If a message is found to be error-free, then it is routed to one of five destinations, each being chosen with equal probability. These five destinations are connected to the switching centre by five separate communications lines with different speeds. The transmission times of these outgoing messages are exponentially distributed with respective means $1/\mu_3$, $1/\mu_4$, $1/\mu_5$, $1/\mu_6$, $1/\mu_7$. Given that the source message traffic is Poisson with rate λ, determine the average total delay experienced by a typical message in flowing through the network.

6. Show that for a K-job cyclic queueing network consisting of N identical exponential single server nodes, the mean number of jobs enqueued to each node is given by K/N.

CHAPTER 8

Operational Analysis

8.1 Introduction

In the foregoing chapters, we have been primarily using a probabilistic description of system behaviour. In this chapter we are going to present a different, essentially non-probabilistic, approach for assessing system performance. The majority of the results in this section are, in fact, derivable from a probabilistic analysis, but it does represent a novel point of view to a familiar situation. The present approach, called *operational analysis*, is primarily measurement based, and instead of manipulating random variables, it manipulates the data collected from empirical observations. Since operational analysis operates on concrete experimental data, it is not only easier to understand, but also renders the testing of the validity of assumptions much more straightforward than in the probabilistic case; e.g. testing whether the input into a queue conforms to a Poisson process can be quite involved, and in any case relies on empirical observations. The basic building blocks of operational analysis are *operational variables*; these are quantities which can be either directly measured or computed from measured quantities. The aim of operational analysis is to establish relationships among operational variables, often with the help of suitable assumptions which can be tested experimentally.

8.2 Fundamental Operational Laws and Theorems

Since operational analysis is concerned with observational data, there is an observation time period associated with the operational variables. An operational variable is a variable which stands for the value of some quantity of interest associated with the observation period. An operational variable can be either basic or derived. Basic operational variables correspond to quantities which are directly obtained during the observation period (i.e. the raw data), while derived operational variables correspond to quantities computed from the basic quantities. For an arbitrary service node, one may have the following basic quantities.

T = the length of the observation period,
A = the total number of arrivals during the observation period,
B = the total amount of time that the system is busy during the observation period,

C = the number of job completions during the observation period,

W = the job-time product, which is obtained by summing the durations of all jobs spent in the node during the observation period.

From these, one may compute the following derived quantities.

I = A/T, the input rate,
H = C/T, the output rate,
U = B/T, the utilization,
J = W/T, the mean number of jobs in the system,
S = B/C, the (conceptual) mean service time (*Note.* this corresponds to the ordinary mean service time if the node is a single server node)
R = W/C, the (conceptual) mean response time (*Note.* this corresponds to the ordinary mean response time if the observation period commences and ends with an empty system).

Since both U and HS equal B/T, the following equation always holds:

$$U = HS \qquad (8.2.1)$$

in all observation periods. Since the validity of this equality stems from the definition of the derived variables and is independent of the actual values observed, it is called an operational identity or *operational law*. The particular identity above is known as the *utilization law*. Supposing the number of arrivals and departures during the observation period are the same (i.e. $A = C$)—a condition known as *flow balance*—then we have $I = H$ and the utilization law becomes

$$U = IS. \qquad (8.2.2)$$

Unlike an operational identity, the above would not hold for all observation periods but holds only for those with flow balance. Since it holds only under certain restrictions on the operational variables (in this case $A = C$) which may sometimes be violated, it is called an *operational theorem*. We recognize, from Section 3.3, that this is really the operational counterpart of the familiar stochastic relation $\rho = \lambda \bar{X}$.

From the definitions, we also find that both J and HR are equal to W/T for all observation periods; i.e.

$$J = HR \qquad (8.2.3)$$

which is also an operational identity and is known as *Little's law*. Likewise, under flow balance this becomes $J = IR$ which is, of course, the operational counterpart of Little's formula.

Example 8.1 During an observation period of $T = 1$ hour, it is found that the number of job arrivals and departures are the same and equal 160, and

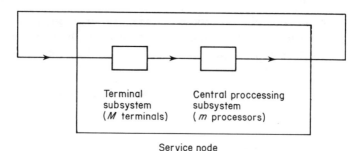

Service node

FIGURE 8.1.   An interactive system

the system is busy for 40 minutes. The job-time product W is found to be 800 job-minutes. Determine (a) the average response time, (b) the average queue length, and (c) the system utilization. Does the relationship $J = IR$ hold here?

Solution.   The system input and output rates are both 2.7 jobs per second. The utilization is simply $40/60 = 67\%$. The average response time is $800/160 = 5$ seconds, and the average queue length is $800/60 = 13.3$ jobs. The relationship $J = IR$ holds here because the system satisfies the condition of flow balance. □

The conditions of flow balance stipulate that the number of arrivals and departures must balance during the observation period, and this is so if the initial number of jobs in the system at the beginning of the period is the same as the final number of jobs in the system at the expiration of the period; for instance, if the observation period commences and ends with an empty system, then we necessarily have flow balance. Flow balance is equivalent to the condition that the input and output rates are the same; as we have seen in the previous chapter, this is similar to the consequence of Burke's theorem and holds if the service node is an exponential one in the probabilistic case. It is interesting to note that while it is relatively trivial to verify flow balance, it is not so straightforward to verify that service times are exponentially distributed.

Next, we consider an interactive system consisting of M user terminals together with a central processing subsystem of user terminals. As explained in Section 6.5, the mean inter-submission time relating to a given user terminal is made up of a mean think time Z and a mean response time R. Here, we shall incorporate the M user terminals into the central processing subsystem to form a single service node as shown in Fig. 8.1. We note that, since a job completed at the central processing subsystem is immediately fed back to the terminal subsystem, we always have flow balance for the service node so defined. Here, the job-time product can be written as $W = C(Z + R)$ since each entry into the node spends an average amount of time $Z + R$ there. The ratio W/T of course yields the mean number of jobs in the node, which is always M, i.e. we have $W/T = M$. Substituting $C(Z + R)$ for W, and solving for R, we obtain

$$R = M/H - Z, \qquad (8.2.4)$$

which is of course the operational analogue of the interactive response time formula (6.5.6).

Example 8.2 Consider a 24-terminal interactive system. Supposing it is given that the mean think time is 30 seconds, and the mean response time is 2 seconds, determine the system output.

Solution. Solving for H in (8.2.4), we have $H = M/(R + Z) = 24/(2 + 30) = 24/32$. Thus the system output is 0.75 per second. □

It is worth pointing out that (8.2.4) is more general than (6.5.6) because the former is applicable to an arbitrary central processing subsystem—which may possibly be a queueing network in itself, while the latter only caters for a single processor in the central processing subsystem. We also note that the detailed structure of the central processing subsystem such as the number of processors inside it does not explicitly enter into the final formula because these factors are implicitly reflected in the job completion rate: in the case of a multiprocessor situation, the number of job completions C in the observation period is greater than that in the case of a single processor.

8.3 Queueing Networks

In this section, we consider the behaviour of an N-node queueing network during an observation period of length T. We shall adopt much the same notation as in the previous section except that we need to identify the operational variables associated with each node to specify the appropriate inter-node routing information. The basic quantities for the given observation period are for $i, j = 1, 2, \ldots, N$

$A(i)$ = total number of request arrivals to node i,

$B(i)$ = the total amount of time that node i is observed to be busy,

$C(i, j)$ = number of request completions at node i which requires service at node j next,

$W(i)$ = the job-time product at node i, which is the sum of the durations of all jobs spent in node i during the observation period.

Furthermore, to cater for external arrivals and departures we add a conceptual node 0 to signify the external wórld; for $i > 0$, $C(0, i)$ signifies the number of external arrivals to node i, while $C(i, 0)$ signifies the number of external departures from node i. We shall denote the total number of external arrivals and departures respectively by $A(0)$ and $C(0)$; i.e.

$$A(0) = \sum_{i=1}^{N} C(0, i),$$

$$C(0) = \sum_{i=1}^{N} C(i, 0).$$

Likewise the total number of arrivals and completions at node i for $i > 0$ are respectively

$$A(i) = \sum_{j=0}^{N} C(j, i),$$

$$C(i) = \sum_{j=0}^{N} C(i, j).$$

From these basic quantities, we can compute

$U(i) = B(i)/T$, the utilization at node i, $i > 0$,
$S(i) = B(i)/C(i)$, the conceptual mean service time at node $i, i > 0$,
$R(i) = W(i)/C(i)$, the conceptual mean response time at node $i, i > 0$,
$J(i) = W(i)/T$, the mean number of jobs at node $i, i > 0$,
$H(i) = C(i)/T$, the output rate from node $i, i \geqslant 0$.

We shall describe the network as satisfying the condition of flow balance if the condition of flow balance holds at each of its $N + 1$ node for the observation period; i.e. $A(i) = C(i)$ for $i = 0, \ldots, N$. Under flow balance, $H(i)$ is the same as the input to node i, and will be referred to as the throughput for node i. Unless otherwise stated, we shall assume in the rest of this chapter that the network satisfies the flow balance condition. In addition to the above derived quantities, we find it useful to define

$q(i, j) = C(i, j)/C(i)$, the routing frequency from node i to node j,
$V(i) = C(i)/C(0)$, the visit ratio which measures the average number of times node i is visited by a job.

For individual nodes flow balance means, for $j > 0$,

$$A(j) = \sum_{i=0}^{N} C(i, j) = \sum_{i=0}^{N} C(j, i) = C(j),$$

which on combining with the definition of $C(0)$ and defining $C(0, 0)$ to be 0 we may write

$$C(j) = \sum_{i=0}^{N} C(i, j), \quad j = 0, 1, 2, \ldots, N. \tag{8.3.1}$$

Applying this to the definition of the routing frequency, we obtain the so-called *flow balance equations*

$$H(j) = \sum_{i=0}^{N} H(i)q(i,j), \qquad j = 0, \ldots, N.$$

The visit ratio could also be written in terms of $H(i)$ as $V(i) = H(i)/H(0)$ or

$$H(i) = V(i)H(0).$$

This is called the *forced flow law* which relates the throughput or 'flow' at node i to the overall network throughput $H(0)$.

Example 8.3 Suppose the system throughput is known to be three jobs a second and each job requires an average of four disk I/Os, determine the disk throughput.

Solution. Here $H(0) = 3$, and $V(i) = 4$. Thus from the forced flow law, the disk throughput is $3 \times 4 = 12$ requests per second. ∇

Dividing both sides of the flow balance equations by $H(0)$, we obtain the so-called visit ratio equations

$$V(0) = 1$$

$$V(j) = q(0,j) + \sum_{i=1}^{N} V(i)q(i,j), \qquad j = 1, \ldots, N.$$

The mean total response time R for the entire network could be expressed in terms of the visit ratios. Applying Little's law to the network as a whole, we have

$$R = J/H(0) \tag{8.3.2}$$

where J denotes the mean total number of jobs in the network for the observation period in question, which can be written as

$$J = J(1) + \cdots + J(N), \tag{8.3.3}$$

with $J(i)$ denoting the mean number of jobs at node i. Applying Little's formula to individual nodes, we have for the mean response time at node

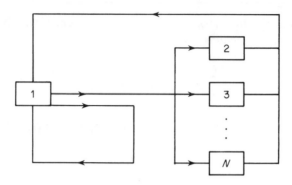

FIGURE 8.2.   Central server model

$$R(i) = J(i)/H(i). \tag{8.3.4}$$

Substituting (8.3.3) and (8.3.4) into (8.3.2) we obtain the so-called *general response time law*

$$R = \sum_{i=1}^{N} V(i)R(i).$$

In deriving this law, we have not made use of the flow balance assumption, so that it holds even if job flow is not balanced.

Example 8.4   Consider a two-node network with overall average response time of 20 seconds. The visit ratios are given to be $V(1) = 3$, $V(2) = 4$. It is observed that the average response time at node one is twice that of node 2. Determine the average response time at each node.

Solution.   From the general response time law, we have

$$20 = 6R(2) + 4R(2),$$

which gives $R(2) = 2$ seconds. The average response time at node one is thus 4 seconds.   □

8.4   Bottleneck Analysis for Closed Queueing Networks

Closed queueing network is useful in representing a wide variety of situations. Consider a model of multiprogramming systems shown in Fig. 8.2 consisting of N nodes and a fixed number of K partitions. Node 1 represents the CPU, and the remaining nodes represent I/O devices. New jobs entering the network always commence with some CPU processing and then circulates in the system alternating between I/O and CPU services before eventually leaving via the CPU node; the possibility that a job requiring only a single CPU burst followed by immediate departure is not excluded. Whenever a job leaves, it is assumed that a new job immediately enters the network to take its place, so that the number of jobs in the network remains constant and equals K. Since the number of jobs in the network is constant, it can be regarded as a closed network; a job departure from the CPU need not be regarded as an external departure—we may regard the departing job and its successor to be *conceptually* the same job requiring two successive bursts of CPU service. The closed queueing network model of multiprogramming in Fig. 8.2 is first studied by Buzen (1971) and is called the *central server model*. The interactive system of Fig. 8.1, too, can be regarded as a closed queueing network because the output from the combined central processing and terminal node is directly fed back to it. In general, a closed queueing network may be viewed as an open network in which the system output is immediately recycled back as input so that the concept of system throughout here remains meaningful.

In a closed queueing network, there is a tendency for jobs to accumulate at the slow service nodes so that by improving the performance of these nodes, a smoother job flow within the network could be achieved. Consider the relative service demands of a closed network with a single server at each node. From the utilization law and the definition of the visit ratio, we can write

$$U(i)/U(j) = V(i)S(i)/V(j)S(j). \qquad (8.4.1)$$

The product $V(i)S(i)$ can be regarded as the total service demand by a job from node i and is denoted by $D(i)$. Suppose we measure the utilization of different nodes relative to a prescribed node—say node 1—then denoting the relative utilization $U(i)/U(1)$ by $U(i)^*$, we have on taking $j = 1$ in (8.4.1),

$$U(i)^* \propto D(i). \qquad (8.4.2)$$

If the total service demand $D(i)$ from node i remains unchanged and the number of jobs K in the network increases, then those nodes with the highest relative utilization are the first to achieve 100% utilization. A node with a utilization of approximately 100% is referred to as *saturated*; not all nodes are capable of saturation, however, because if, say, most of the jobs are accumulated at a certain node, the remaining nodes may not have enough jobs to flow through them to enable the attainment of a 100% utilization. A node which is capable of saturating as $K \to \infty$ is called a *bottleneck*. Since saturation is dependent on the relative utilization, every closed queueing network has at least one bottleneck, namely those with the highest relative utilization. If we use the index c to signify a bottleneck node—there can be several of these in a network—then we have

$$U(c)^* = \max \{U(1)^*, U(2)^*, \ldots, U(N)^*\},$$

and from (8.4.2) this condition can also be expressed as (on dividing the above by the constant of proportionality in (8.4.1))

$$D(c) = \max \{D(1), \ldots, D(N)\}. \qquad (8.4.3)$$

If the number of jobs in the network is large (i.e. $K \to \infty$), then eventually

$U(c) \to 1$. The system throughput $H(0)$, by the forced flow law, is $H(0) = H(c)/V(c)$, and by the utilization law $H(c) \to 1/S(c)$ so that we can conclude that the maximum system throughput $\to 1/D(c)$ as $K \to \infty$. We shall denote the maximum possible network throughput $1/D(c)$ by H_{max}. For $K > 0$, the minimum network throughput, denoted by H_{min}, by Little's law is attained when there is only a single job in the network, i.e. $H_{min} = 1/R_{min}$, where R_{min} denotes the response time corresponding to $K = 1$. Since there is only a single job in the network, there exists no contention delay and all the resources are immediately available for use by the job in question; the response time R_{min} is thus the minimum possible and is simply equal to the total service demand, i.e.

$$R_{min} = D(1) + \cdots + D(N),$$

and so

$$H_{min} = 1/[D(1) + \cdots + D(N)].$$

Thus, when there are $0 < K < \infty$ jobs in the network, the corresponding network throughput $H(0)$ has limits given by

$$H_{min} = 1/[D(1) + \cdots + D(N)] \leq H(0) \leq H_{max} = 1/D(c). \quad (8.4.4)$$

When there exists k jobs is the network, then under the most ideal condition where they do not interfere with one another, the resultant throughput is $H(0) = kH_{min}$; the second inequality in (8.4.4) implies that $H(0) \leq H_{max}$, so that when $k > K^* = H_{max}/H_{min}$, this necessarily means that $kH_{min} > H(0)$. This means that when

$$k > K^* = [D(1) + \ldots + D(N)]/D(c),$$

the actual network throughput $H(0)$ is necessarily less than that of kH_{min}, so that the above ideal conditions of no interference cannot be maintained, and contention interference is unavoidable. This critical workload K^* is termed the saturation point of the network.

Example 8.5 Consider a three-node closed network with $D(1) = 3$ seconds, $D(2) = 10$ seconds and $D(3) = 7$ seconds. Determine (a) the system bottleneck, (b) the maximum throughput, (c) the minimum throughput, and (d) the critical number of jobs exceeding which interference is inevitable.

Solution. Since $D(2)$ is the highest, node 2 is thus the system bottleneck. The maximum network throughput is $1/D(2) = 0.1$. The minimum network throughput is $1/20 = 0.05$. Thus the critical number of jobs K^* is $20/10 = 2$. □

In the case of an interactive system, applying (8.4.4) to the interactive response time formula, we have for the mean response time

$$R = M/H(0) - Z \geq M/H_{max} - Z,$$

so that

$$R \geqslant MD(c) - Z.$$

For sufficiently large M, the right hand side necessarily exceeds R_{min}; i.e.

$$MD(c) - Z > R_{min} = 1/[D(1) + \cdots + D(N)].$$

More precisely, if M exceeds the critical value

$$M^* = [R_{min} + Z]/D(c),$$

then we must have $R > R_{min}$. This states that when the number of active terminals M exceeds M^*, contention is certain to occur in the central subsystem.

It is worth pointing out that reducing the total service demand of a node (e.g. by upgrading the associated device to a faster one) which is not a bottleneck would not affect the maximum network throughput because the upper bound $H_{max} = 1/D(c)$ is unchanged. However, lowering service demand for the bottleneck raises the upper bound H_{max} provided $D(c)$ remains the largest; excessive improvement there will move the bottleneck to another node so that additional improvement will bring about no further change to the maximum throughput.

8.5 Summary

In this chapter, we have concentrated on the method of operational analysis, which is primarily an empirical, non-probabilistic approach to the study of queueing networks. It makes use of operational variables, which are directly measured or derived from observed quantities. An operational law represents a relationship among the operational variables which is always valid, irrespective of the individual values of the operational variables, and is a direct result of the definition of the operational variables. Among the common operational laws are the utilization law, Little's law, and the forced flow law. An operational theorem, on the other hand, is valid only when certain constraints are imposed on the operational variables, and accordingly is not valid for all observation periods. A common constraint is flow balance, which requires the number of arrivals and departures in the observation period to be the same. We have also used operational analysis to study the behaviour of closed queueing networks. We discover that bottlenecks are always present in such networks, and by analyzing the characteristics of bottlenecks, it is possible to obtain useful performance and workload features of the network.

8.6 Exercises

1. During an observation period of 3 hours, it is found that the number of jobs arrivals and departures are the same and equals 360, and the system is busy for 110 minutes. The job-time product W is found to be 1200 job-minutes,

Determine (a) the average response time, (b) the average queue length, and (c) the system utilization.

   2. Consider a 17-terminal interactive system. Supposing it is given that the mean think time is 20 seconds, and the mean response time is 3 seconds, determine the system output.

   3. Suppose it is given that the system throughput is 10 jobs/second and each job requires an average of two printer I/Os and four disk I/Os. Determine the printer and disk throughputs.

   4. Consider a three-node network with overall average response time of 20 seconds. The visit ratios are given to be $V(1) = V(3) = 3$, $V(2) = 4$. It is observed that the average response time at node 1 is twice that of node 2, and that the average response time at node 2 is a quarter of that of node 3. Determine the average response time at each node.

   5. Consider a four-node closed network with $D(1) = 1$ second, $D(2) = 11$ seconds, $D(3) = 15$ seconds, and $D(4) = 12$ seconds. Determine (a) the system bottleneck, (b) the maximum throughput, (c) the minimum throughput, and (d) the critical number of jobs exceeding which interference is inevitable. Which device would you consider upgrading in order to improve the performance of the network?

CHAPTER 9

Database and I/O Subsystem Performance

9.1 Introduction

One of the chief reasons for installing computer systems in business and government organizations is the amount of data that a computer can handle, and the speed and flexibility with which the data can be accessed. Effective data management often constitutes a major function of these installations. It is generally impractical to keep large files and databases in main memory as it is volatile and its storage capacity is often limited. Tape storage is unsuitable for online retrieval and is restricted to mainly sequential file organizations; it is inflexible and incapable of handling the complex data structuring requirements of modern databases.

To support speedy flexible data access requirements, the commonest storage medium is the magnetic disk, either with fixed head or movable head. As these devices continuously rotate at a constant speed, the read/write head very often has to wait for the correct record to come under it before data transfer can take place. This delay is often referred to as the *rotational delay* or *latency*, and is applicable to both movable head and fixed head disks. In the case of the movable head disk, a further delay, called the *seek time*, is often required to position the read/write head at the correct cylinder. In the first part of this chapter, we shall look at models and formulae associated with the performance of these direct access storage devices, since they have a direct influence on database efficiency.

Unless otherwise stated, the traffic input to these devices will be taken to follow a Poisson process. Throughout this chapter, the following notations are used:

λ : rate of request arrival to the device
L : the latency
U : the disk seek distance
S : the disk seek time
T : time for one complete disk revolution
D : time taken to transfer a data block from the disk, excluding any seek time or latency delay
X : the device service time.

For the fixed head disk, its service time is $L + D$; for the movable head disk, its service time is $S + L + D$. A detailed study of these service components together with their possible inter-dependence is given in Sections 9.3 and 9.4. In Section 9.5, we shall look at common means of obtaining the best performance from databases by applying some simple rules concerning file buffering and data placement. Finally, in Section 9.6, we shall examine models for effective database maintenance and reorganization.

9.2 Basic Storage Structures

We find it necessary to distinguish two main data storage formats on these devices: the *fixed length record format* and the *variable length record format*. In the former, the time required to transfer a *data block* or *physical record* is constant, and there exists no variability among record lengths. In the latter, the data transfer time is variable, and there exists variability among record lengths. A physical record forms the basic unit of data transferred between the disk and main memory, and is made up of one or more *logical records* grouped together. As a physical record corresponds to a given angular position on the circular disk surface, we sometimes find it convenient, especially with the fixed length record format, to refer to a given arc on the disk which holds a physical record as a *sector*.

9.3 The Fixed Head Disk

In this section, we consider the performance of the fixed head disk operating under the FIFO and the shortest-latency-time-first (SLTF) scheduling rules. The SLTF rule aims to minimize the latency delay under which service selection is based on the latency time: when the read/write head becomes free it selects for transmission the record with the shortest latency delay relative to its current position. The FIFO rule, of course, selects for transmission the record associated with a request which has the earliest arrival time.

9.3.1   *The FIFO Fixed Head Disk with Variable Length Records*

Here, we consider situations where variability exists among record lengths. The analysis here is relatively straightforward and consists of the routine application of the Pollaczek–Khintchine formula once the service characteristics are identified. The service time X is simply the sum of the latency L and the record transfer time D, i.e.

$$X = L + D.$$

Since the record lengths are variable, L and D can be regarded as independent—which is not the case when the record lengths are fixed (see Section

9.3.2)—and L may further be taken to be uniformly distributed over the interval $[0, T)$. Thus the first and second moments of X are

$$\bar{X} = T/2 + \bar{D},$$
$$\overline{X^2} = \overline{L^2} + \bar{D}T + \overline{D^2} = T^2/3 + \bar{D}T + \overline{D^2}.$$

The mean response time $\bar{R}$ under Poisson input with rate λ is therefore, from the Pollaczek–Khintchine formula,

$$\bar{R} = \frac{\lambda(T^2/3 + T\bar{D} + \overline{D^2})}{2[1 - \lambda(T/2 + \bar{D})]} + T/2 + \bar{D},$$

where we have assumed that the system is stable, i.e. $\lambda\bar{X} < 1$. The utilization of the device is $\lambda(T/2 + \bar{D})$.

9.3.2 The FIFO Fixed Head Disk with Fixed Length Records

Here, we consider situations where there is no variation among record lengths so that D is a constant. Suppose there are N physical records to a track so that $ND = T$, and that each record is equally likely to be accessed. The analysis here is more complicated than that for the fixed head disk with variable length records because it is now necessary to distinguish between two types of requests: initiators and non-initiators (see Section 4.2.2). For non-initiators, the elapsed time between successive request completions, which is equal to the service time, must be in integral multiples of D; there is thus a dependence between L and D. If X denotes the service time of non-initiators, its distribution is

$$\Pr[X = nD] = 1/N, \qquad n = 1, 2, \ldots, N.$$

Its mean is

$$\bar{X} = (1 + 2 + \cdots + N)D/N = (N + 1)D/2,$$

and likewise, its second moment is

$$\overline{X^2} = (N + 1)(2N + 1)D^2/6.$$

For initiators, however, their service time need not be in integral multiples of D because arrivals could take place at any time, not necessarily at record boundaries. If H denotes the service time of initiators, then H consists of a rotation delay V to the first record boundary, then followed by a delay similar to that for non-initiators to locate and transfer the required record. That is

$$H = V + X.$$

In Leung and Choo (1984b), it is shown that the probability density of V is, for $0 < t < D$,

$$\lambda \exp[-\lambda(D - t)]/[1 - \exp(-\lambda D)].$$

Evaluating the mean and second moment of H using the above and substituting them into the generalized Pollaczek–Khintchine formula, we obtain, after substantial simplification, the mean response time

$$\bar{R} = (N+2)D/2 + (N+1)(2N+1)\lambda D^2/\{6[2 - \lambda D(N+1)]\},$$

the mean service time can be shown to be

$$\bar{X} = \{1/[1 - \exp(-\lambda D)] - 1/(\lambda D) + (N+1)/2\}[1 - \exp(-\lambda D)]/\lambda,$$

and the device utilization is

$$\rho = 1 - [1/(\lambda D) - (N+1)/2][1 - \exp(-\lambda D)].$$

For sufficiently small D (i.e. $D \simeq 0$) then the distinction between initiators and non-initiators becomes insignificant and the service time is $\approx T/2$, so that the device utilization can be approximated by $\lambda T/2$.

9.3.3 The SLTF Fixed Head Disk with Fixed Length Records

Although the analysis of the SLTF fixed head disk with fixed length records may appear to be quite involved, it is actually no more difficult than that for the FIFO rule. Here, instead of focusing on the disk queue as a whole, attention is focused on the individual sector queue because whenever a sector is passed under the read/write head, the request at the head of the associated queue, if non-empty, is always processed regardless of its relative time of arrival compared with requests enqueued at other sectors. The service sequence resulting from such a procedure is precisely that for the SLTF rule. Here, it is also necessary to distinguish between initiators and non-initiators. The service requirements of non-initiators for a sector queue is evidently the constant T. The service characteristics of the initiators can be determined in much the same way as for the FIFO disk (but computationally more laborious); the mean service and response times relating to a sector queue are shown in Leung and Choo (1984b) to be

$$\bar{X} = \{(\lambda D - 1)[1 - \exp(-\lambda D)]/[(\lambda D)\exp\{-\lambda(T - D)/N\}] + 1\}N/\lambda,$$
$$\bar{R} = \{1/2 + 1/N + \lambda D/[2(1 - \lambda D)]\}T.$$

It is interesting to note that this system is highly responsive to workload demand: when a large number of requests are present, the latency delay to reach the nearest request is small, so that the request service time here is not constant but regulates itself in accordance with the load. The device utilization is found in Leung and Choo (1984b) to be

$$\rho = 1 - \exp(-\lambda D)[\exp(\lambda D) - 1]^N[1 - \lambda D]^N/(\lambda D)^N;$$

and the service time for the device queue (as opposed to the sector queue) is

$$1/\lambda - \exp(-\lambda D)[\exp(\lambda D) - 1]^N[1 - \lambda D]^N/[\lambda(\lambda D)^N].$$

It can be shown that for $D \simeq 0$, the device utilization can be approximated by

$$\rho \simeq 1 - \exp(-\lambda T/2),$$

which is always < 1 for all values of λ, so that the possibility of device overloading in such a situation could be ignored. The same, however, cannot be said for the FIFO case, since $\lambda T/2$ is eventually > 1 for sufficiently large λ. The mean device service time here when D is small is $\simeq [1 - \exp(-\lambda T/2)]/\lambda$.

9.3.4 *The SLTF Fixed Head Disk with Variable Length Records*

The solution of this system is extremely difficult because records could commence at any point on the track, and no exact closed-form expression is available for the mean response time. An approximation (see Fuller (1975)) for the mean response time which is partly based on empirical simulation is

$$\bar{R} = T/2 + \lambda \bar{D} T/[1 - \lambda \bar{D}] + 0.37T[\lambda \bar{D}/(1 - \lambda \bar{D})]^{3/2} + \bar{D}.$$

9.4 The Movable Head Disk

The main difference of the movable head disk and the fixed head disk is the presence of an extra service delay, namely, the seek time. In this section, we shall consider the movable head disk operating under the FIFO and SCAN sequencing rules. With the SCAN rule the read/write head scans across the cylinders in a given direction, servicing requests as they are encountered irrespective of their time of arrival. When there are no more requests ahead, it reverses the direction of the scan again servicing requests as they are encountered. With the FIFO rule, no attempt is made to minimize the seek delay, so that the service time of a request does not depend on the number of requests in the queue. With the SCAN rule, however, the service time of a given request, like that for the SLTF fixed head disk, is dependent on the number of requests in the queue, since it attempts to reduce the seek delay per request; and in doing so it reduces also the amount of head movement and the device utilization.

9.4.1 *The Random Seek Distribution*

Since the seek time is determined by the seek distance, we now examine the distribution of the seek distance. We shall focus our attention on the random seek case where each cylinder on the disk is equally likely to be accessed and the cylinder position of successive requests are independent. We assume that the total number of cylinders on the disk is C, and that C is sufficiently large so that the disk surface may be approximated by the continuous interval $(0, C)$. The seek distance U of a request is dependent on both the position of the previous request A and the position of the present one B, each of which is assumed to be uniformly distributed on $(0, C)$. Diagrammatically, the

FIGURE 9.1. The seek distance

situation may be represented in Fig. 9.1 where for concreteness we assume that $A < B$. Because of our assumption that the points A and B are uniformly distributed over the surface $(0, C)$, it is not difficult to see, from the symmetry of the situation, that the lengths of the intervals $(0, A)$, (A, B) and (B, C) have the same distribution; the length of the interval (A, B) is of course the seek distance. We shall compute the seek distance distribution by concentrating on the interval $(0, A)$, whose length can be denoted by U. Now $U > u$ means that both A and B fall on the sub-interval (u, C): the probability that one of them falls on (u, C) is, by uniformity, $(C - u)/C$ so that the probability $\Pr[U > u]$ is simply the product $[(C - u)/C]^2$, i.e.

$$\Pr[U > u] = [(C - u)/C]^2,$$

so that the cumulative distribution function of U is

$$1 - [(C - u)/C]^2, \qquad (9.4.1)$$

yielding the following probability density for U:

$$2(C - u)/C^2, \qquad 0 < u < C. \qquad (9.4.2)$$

From this the mean and variance of U can be obtained

$$\bar{U} = C/3,$$

$$\mathrm{Var}(U) = C^2/18.$$

If the seek characteristic—i.e. the relationship between the seek time and the seek distance—is linear and of the form

$$S = a + bU, \qquad (9.4.3)$$

where a and b are constants, then

$$\bar{S} = a + bC/3,$$
$$\mathrm{Var}(S) = (bC)^2/18.$$

For example, the IBM 3330 disk may be approximated by a linear seek function with $a = 10$ and $b = 0.1$, if S is measured in milliseconds.

9.4.2   The FIFO Disk with Variable Length Records

Like the FIFO fixed head disk with variable length records, the analysis of this system is relatively straightforward once the service characteristics have been identified. The service time X here consists of (1) the seek time S, (2) the latency L and (3) the record transfer time D. Here, we assume a positive value for the variance of D, i.e. $\mathrm{Var}(D) > 0$, and so these three components are all independent. As in the FIFO fixed head disk with variable length records, L may be taken to be uniformly distributed over the interval $[0, T)$. It therefore remains to incorporate the seek time distribution. Adopting the linear seek characteristic (9.4.3) of the previous section, and combining it with those of the remaining service components, followed by substitution into the Pollaczek–Khintchine formula, we obtain the mean I/O response time

$$\bar{R} = \frac{\rho \bar{X}\{1 + [(bC)^2/18 + T^2/12 + \mathrm{Var}(D)]/\bar{X}^2\}}{2(1 - \rho)} + \bar{X},$$

where $\rho = \lambda \bar{X}$ and $\bar{X} = a + bC/3 + T/2 + \bar{D}$.

Example 9.1 Suppose it is given that $\bar{D} = 1$, and that the data blocks are exponentially distributed. Assuming a value for $T = 16.7$ ms, determine the I/O response time in randomly accessing a file of size 67 cylinders stored on the IBM 3330 when the traffic intensity is 0.6.

Solution Using the values for a and b given above for the IBM 3330, and a value for $C = 67$, we have $X = 10 + 2.2 + 8.4 + 1 = 21.6$. Since the data blocks are exponentially distributed, $\mathrm{Var}(D) = 1$. Substituting these values into the above formula, the mean response time is equal to $[0.6 \times 21.6\{1 + (2.5 + 23.2 + 1)/466.6\}]/0.8 + 21.6 = 38.7$ ms. $\square$

9.4.3 The SCAN Disk With Variable Length Records

An exact analysis of this situation is difficult, but the mean response time for the SCAN disk with variable length records and a linear seek characteristic of the form (9.4.3) when $C \gg 1$ is shown in Oney (1975) to be

$$\bar{R} \approx \frac{\lambda\{T^2 + 12[\mathrm{Var}(D) + K^2]\}(1 + \lambda K/C)}{24[1 - (\lambda K)^2/C]} + \frac{0.71bC(1 - \lambda K/C)}{1 - \lambda K},$$

where $K = a + T/2 + \bar{D}$.

9.4.4 The FIFO Disk with Fixed Length Records

In this situation, there exists a dependence between the seek time S and the rotational latency L, since their sum must necessarily be in integral multiples of the basic block duration D. A detailed analysis of this situation, which is based on the generalized Pollaczek–Khintchine formula, may be found in Leung and Choo (1982). For full-track blocked data, i.e. $D = T$, the mean response time is given by

$$\bar{R} = p_0 y_1 + (1 - p_0)x_1 + \lambda p_0[y_2(1 - \lambda x_1) + \lambda y_1 x_2]/[2(1 - \lambda x_1)^2],$$

where x_k is given by

$$\sum_{n=1}^{\infty} [(n+1)T]^k [F(nT) - F((n-1)T)],$$

with $F(.)$ representing the seek time distribution; y_m is given by the mth moment of $Y = Z + T$, which represents the service time of initiators, with

$$\overline{Z^m} = \lambda[1 - \exp(-\lambda T)]^{-1} \sum_{k=1}^{\infty} \int_{(k-1)T}^{kT} t^m \exp[-\lambda(kT - t)][F(t) - F(t - T)]dt,$$

and

$$p_0 = (1 - \lambda x_1)/[1 - \lambda x_1 + \lambda y_1].$$

Example 9.2 Assuming a value for $T = 16.7$ ms, determine, using the formula in this section, the I/O response time in randomly accessing a file of size 67 cylinders stored on the IBM 3330 when the traffic intensity is 0.6, and the data are full-track blocked. How does the result compared with that obtained from the response time formula in Section 9.3.2?

Solution Using the formulae given above and applying (9.4.3) with $a = 10$ and $b = 0.1$, we obtain $\bar{R} = 59.39$ ms. The result from the response time formula in Section 9.4.2 is 75.98 ms, assuming $\text{Var}(D) = 0$ there; this latter result shows an error of 27.9%. This is due to the fact that the dependence between the seek time and rotational delay is ignored in the formula in Section 9.4.2. □

9.5 File Buffering and Locality Referencing

As mentioned earlier, the database component forms the heart of many practical information systems, and efficient data management often constitutes the reason for existence of many commercial and scientific data processing systems. Thus, speeding up the database subsystem of an information system is likely to yield significant performance benefits.

We have already seen that the performance of the disk system can be considerably improved by adopting suitable scheduling strategies to reduce the seek time and rotational delay. This generally has a beneficial effect on the database system as data records are normally held on disks. Suitably balancing the device loading (described in Chapter 13) also helps to improve efficiency.

For sequential file access, suitably buffering the data blocks increases the CPU and I/O overlap and reduces delay: by the use of *double buffering*—i.e. allocating two data block storage slots in main memory instead of one—the transfer of a second block into main memory may take place while the first data block is being processed by the CPU. Depending on the relative times

taken for I/O transfer and CPU processing of a data block, sometimes multiple
buffering (i.e. providing possibly more than two buffers) may further improve
performance.

Example 9.3 (Double buffering)   Suppose it is given that the average time
required to transfer a block of data from a given I/O device to main memory
is 30 ms, and the time required to process a data block by the CPU is on
average 10 ms. Assuming no interference from other jobs, determine the
approximate elapsed time in processing a sequential file of 1000 records using
(a) single buffering, and (b) double buffering.

Solution   In the case of single buffering, there is no overlap between the
I/O transfer and CPU processing of a data block, so that the elapsed time
required for transferring and processing a data block is 30 + 10 = 40 ms. The
total time taken for 1000 records is therefore 40 seconds. In the case of double
buffering, the transfer of a data block can proceed in parallel with the
processing of a previous one, so that I/O transfer can take place continuously
giving a total approximate elapsed time of 30 seconds. Compared with single
buffering, this represents a reduction in elapsed time of 25%.   □

By suitable placement of data on a disk, it is also possible to achieve some
degree of *disk locality referencing*. Localizing disk access is able to counter
excessive arm movement and enhances performance efficiency. In direct
access files, one should placed synonyms and overflow records in close
proximity to the home buckets. In indexed files, the index, home data records,
and overflow records should be placed in the same cylinder. Whenever
possible, related data items in a database, such as those directly linked by
pointer chains, should be stored close to each other. Fragmentation of data
files over non-contiguous locations on a disk, although permitted in many
systems, is generally undesirable, for it destroys locality access. It is therefore
advisable to deliberately inhibit file fragmentation during file creation, which
is enforceable in some systems. More detailed performance analysis of disk
locality referencing are given in Leung and Wolfenden (1983) and Leung
(1983c), and that of storage fragmentation is given in Leung (1982a, 1983a,
1983b). A systematic treatment of data placement considerations may be
found in Wong (1980).

Since I/O transfers are much more time consuming than main memory
access, it is often worthwhile to have frequently required data held in main
memory. For example, the indices of indexed files may be held in main
memory for the duration of the database operation as every random access
to the file may need to refer to them. For time-critical database applications,
the use of specialist hardware is especially effective; using such database
machines, an improvement by a factor of 50 for exhaustive disk searches is
not uncommon (see Leung and Wong (1985)).

Example 9.4 (Disk Locality Referencing)   Consider a disk with the following characteristics: revolution time = 16.7 ms, average seek time = 30 ms. Assuming requests arrive at the rate of 10 requests/second and a block duration of 2 ms, evaluate the potential performance benefits offered by locality referencing in terms of device availability.

Solution   In ideal situations, locality referencing means that no seek time will be incurred in accessing a data block, so that the average time taken to locate and read a given block is half a revolution for latency plus the block reading time, which equals $16.7/2 + 2 = 10.4$ ms. The device utilization is thus $0.01 \times 10.4 = 0.1$ or 10%. If availability is measured in terms of the probability of finding the device idle, then the device availability here is 90%. In the absence of locality referencing, the seek time must be taken into consideration, so that the resultant device utilization is $0.01(10.4 + 30)$ or 40%, which corresponds to an availability of 60%. The benefits imparted by locality refencing is an increase in device availability of 50%.   □

Due to record insertions, deletions, and modifications, the performance of a database system is seldom static. As time goes on, it tends to be disorganized with long overflow chains, out-of-sequence records, and unusable space occupied by logically deleted records. Such disorganization is almost always accompanied by a deterioration in performance. By the use of *distributed free space* within the database, the rate of performance deterioration may be partially checked, since it is possible to place newly inserted records in sequence in their home locations rather than as overflow records. In any case, periodically reorganizing a database system is generally advisable to prevent deterioration to unacceptable levels. Reorganization is able to reduce overflow chains, compact the file into a single area, reclaim wasted space, and restore records to their home locations. In Section 9.6 we shall examine mathematical models of database maintenance.

9.6 Models of Database Reorganization

In this section, we shall examine some simple models of database reorganization similar to those proposed in Shneiderman (1973) and Leung (1986). Suppose the access cost of a database deteriorates linearly with time at a rate β in such a way that, after a time x after the last reorganization, the access cost is given by

$$A(x) = m + \beta x, \qquad (9.6.1)$$

where m and β are positive constants which do not vary from reorganization to reorganization. Immediately after a reorganization, the access cost returns to m but thereafter deteriorates linearly in accordance with (9.6.1) until the next reorganization point. Suppose the total lifespan of the database under consideration is T', the inter-reorganization interval is s, and the cost per reorganization is c. If the database reference rate per unit time v is constant, then the number of database accesses in a small time interval $(t, t + dt)$ is $v \, dt$, with each access incurring a cost of $A(t)$; thus the access cost incurred for each inter-reorganization interval is

$$\int_0^s vA(x) \, dx = v[ms + \beta s^2/2],$$

and the corresponding reorganization cost is simply c. Hence, the total operating cost per inter-reorganization interval is $vms + v\beta s^2/2 + c$. Since the number of reorganizations occurring in the entire lifespan of the database is T'/s, the total operating cost over the entire lifespan of the database is

$$T'[vms + v\beta s^2/2 + c]/s = T'vm + v\beta T's/2 + cT'/s.$$

The optimal reorganization interval s^* may be found by differentiating the above and setting the result to zero. This gives the square root formula

$$s^* = \sqrt{[2c/(v\beta)]}. \tag{9.6.2}$$

We note that if the cost of reorganization cost c is small, then it is economical to carry out reorganization relatively frequently. On the other hand, if the deterioration rate is slow, then it is not necessary to carry out reorganizations too often; likewise, if the database is used infrequently with a small reference rate v, then frequent reorganizations are not called for.

Example 9.5 Consider a database system in which it has been estimated that, in the absence of any reorganization, deterioration occurs in such a way that for every 10 days of operation an additional disk access is incurred. Suppose the database is referenced on average 20 times a day, and that a reorganization requires on average an equivalent of 10 000 disk accesses. Determine how frequently the database should be reorganized.

Solution Taking the number of disk accesses to be the cost unit, the parameters of the present situation are

$$c = 10\,000$$
$$v = 20$$
$$\beta = 0.1.$$

Substituting these into (9.6.2) gives

$$s^* = \sqrt{(20\,000/2)} = 100.$$

Thus the optimal reorganization strategy requires the database to be reorganized once every 100 days. □

Frequently, the deterioration rate is difficult to estimate in practice. We present next a more concrete model which specifically considers the harmful effect of deleted records on database performance. In many database systems,

116

physical deletion of records is not permitted during normal operation: the unwanted records are tentatively flagged as logically deleted while physical removals are performed only when the database is reorganized. As time goes on, the database consists of a mixture of live and dead records which gradually cause it to be fragmented into a random chequer-board pattern with groups of live and dead records alternating one another. Accordingly, the cost of accessing live records increases because of the additional overhead in skipping over the dead ones. In such a situation, the average number of record accesses per reference can be quite excessive when a large number of logically deleted records are present. Here, the purpose of a reorganization is to compact the file by physically removing the logically deleted records while preserving the live ones. This process requires first referencing a record from the database to determine whether or not it has been logically deleted—the associated 'read' cost per record is denoted by c_1—and, if it is not, then transferring it to a new compacted database which replaces the old one—we denote this transfer or 'write' cost per record by c_2. The detailed derivation of the optimal inter-reorganization interval is beyond the scope of the present treatment but can be found in Leung (1986). The associated results, however, are quite simple, with the optimal inter-reorganization interval s^* given by

$$s^* = \sqrt{[2\bar{\tau}(1 + g)/v']},\qquad(9.6.3)$$

where g denotes the relative transfer cost c_2/c_1, $\bar{\tau}$ signifies the mean record lifetime, which is assumed to be exponentially distributed, and v' is the mean reference rate per record. Note that the parameter v' in this model is different from the parameter v in the previous model. Here, we are explicitly considering the status of individual records (i.e. live or dead) and a time-varying database size; it is thus not meaningful to consider the aggregate reference rate v for the sum total of all records in the database. Compared with the previous model, this one is less abstract and more detailed as it explicitly incorporates the database read and write costs, the lifespan of individual records, and their reference characteristics.

Example 9.6 We consider a disk database consisting of fixed length, blocked records operating in a multiprogramming environment, and we assume that cost here can reasonably be measured in terms of the mean access time. We suppose that the database is full-track blocked with a blocking factor of 10, and is stored in a disk with the following characteristics: revolution time = 16.7 ms, average seek time = 30 ms. In this situation, it is not unreasonable to estimate the cost of reading a block by the sum of: average seek time + half a disk revolution for latency + a full revolution for data transfer = 30 + 8.4 + 16.7 = 55.1 ms, so that the cost of reading a record is 55.1/10 = 5.51 ms. Suppose that, for integrity reasons, write verification operations (see Chapter 2) are always incorporated so that an additional disk revolution is necessary in order to complete the writing of a block during reorganization. This gives the cost of writing a block during reorganization to be 55.1 + 16.7 =

71.8 ms, and that of writing a record to be $71.8/10 = 7.18$ ms. The value of the relative transfer cost g accordingly is $7.18/5.51$ or 1.3. Suppose the database is up for 10 hours a day, 7 days a week throughout the year. If the mean record lifetime has been estimated to be about one year, and each record is referenced on the average once a week, then $\bar{\tau} = 52$ and $v' = 1$. From (9.6.3), the database should be reorganized once every $\sqrt{(2 \times 52 \times 2.3)} = 15.5$ weeks, which is 1083 hours of operation or approximately 108 days. If the reference frequency is stepped up to three times a week, then the optimal reorganization interval is dropped to $\sqrt{(2 \times 52 \times 2.3/3)} = 8.9$ weeks, or roughly 62 days. $\square$

9.7 Summary

In this chapter, we have analyzed the the performance of disk storage devices having different hardware characteristics, operating under different scheduling rules, and adopting different storage structures. We have looked at the fixed head and movable head disks, where in the latter an additional seek delay is involved in moving the read/write head to the appropriate cylinder. The scheduling disciplines we have considered include the FIFO, SLTF, and SCAN rules. We have seen that the record format—either fixed length or variable length—has a decisive influence on file performance behaviour, and that different storage formats generally require different queueing models for their analysis. We have also considered performance improvements introduced by efficient data buffering and suitable data placement strategies. Finally, we have introduced models for describing dynamic database deterioration over time, and how such deterioration, which is present in nearly all database systems, may be controlled through the adoption of suitable reorganization procedures.

9.8 Exercises

1. Using arguments similar to those presented in Section 9.4.1, show that for a discrete store with C locations, the average random seek distance is given by $(C^2 - 1)/(3C)$. What are the errors in using the continuous approximation when $C = 100$, 200, and 300?

2. For a movable head disk which rotates at a speed of 3600 rpm, calculate the I/O response time in randomly accessing a file of size 400 cylinders when the traffic intensity is 0.5 and the data are full-track blocked. You may assume that the seek characteristic of the disk is similar to that of the IBM 3330.

3. Suppose it is given that the average time required to transfer a block of data from a given I/O device to main memory is 25 ms, and the time required to process a data block by the CPU is on average 7 ms. Compare the approximate elapsed time in processing a sequential file of 3000 records using (a) double buffering, and (b) triple buffering, assuming no interference from other jobs.

4. Consider the processing of an indexed sequential file stored on a disk with the following characteristics: revolution time = 16.7 ms, average seek time = 30 ms. Assuming file requests arrive at the rate of 5/second, contrast the file response times for the following situations: (a) the index is held on disk; (b) the index is held in main memory. (*Hint*: You may assume that in (a) each file request requires two random disk accesses, and in (b) each file request requires only 1 random disk access, and that the appropriate arrival streams may be approximated by Poisson processes.)

5. Consider a database system in which it has been estimated that, in the ·absence of any reorganization, deterioration occurs in such a way that for every 8 days of operation, an additional disk access is incurred. Suppose the database is referenced on average 12 times a day, and that a reorganization requires on average an equivalent of 5000 disk accesses. Determine how frequently the database should be reorganized.

6. Consider a disk file consisting of variable length, unblocked records. Assume that cost here can reasonably be measured in terms of the number of disk accesses, and that the reading and the writing of each record requires one disk access. Suppose the file is up for 8 hours a day, 5 days a week, giving a total operational time of 40 hours per week. If it is estimated that each live record is referenced on the average twice a week, and that a record remains in the file for typically 13 weeks before it is deleted, determine the optimal reorganization interval for this situation.

CHAPTER 10

Approximations and Time-dependent System Behaviour

10.1 Introduction

The queueing formulae for single node systems presented in earlier chapters has a number of restrictions which limit their practical applicability. The restrictions are

(1) the arrival process must be completely random (i.e. Poisson arrival),
(2) the system has reached a state of equilibrium so that its time-dependent evolution is not of interest.

In addition to these restrictions on the system specification, the results obtained in the main are related to mean values only, which convey very little information on the distributional characteristics of the key performance indices. The main reason why the above restrictions are imposed and more general results are not available is due to the intractability of the problems, which tend to preclude exact closed-form solutions. In this chapter, we consider lifting these restrictions and present more general results concerning the distributional characteristics of some of the performance indices. However, these results, unlike those presented earlier, are inexact and are only approximations which yield varying degrees of accuracy depending on the special features and characters of individual situations.

We first consider the $G/G/1$ system operating in equilibrium and present approximation formulae for the distribution of the waiting time and the queue size using the so-called *diffusion approximation*. In Section 10.2 we shall present a formula giving the time-dependent distribution of the request waiting time, which is also based on the diffusion approximation. Finally in Section 10.3 we shall be concerned with the performance of the $G/G/m$ system, this time using the so-called *heavy traffic approximation*. In this chapter, we shall mostly omit the derivations leading to the appropriate formulae as they tend to be rather intricate and distractive; however, we shall clearly spell out the precise conditions under which the approximations are valid.

10.2   The Equilibrium Waiting Time and Queue Size of the G/G/1 System: Diffusion Approximation

In a single server queueing system, the queue size $Q(t)$ at a given time t are nonnegative integers, and the smallest change to $Q(t)$ accordingly can be either $+1$ (for arrival) or -1 (for departure), the magnitude of which, being unity, is certainly not infinitesimal. Diffusion processes, on the other hand, allow infinitesimal change over time where local changes may be represented by stochastic differential equations; the solutions to these equations are random functions which may be represented as a family of functions over time, so that a particular (random) outcome results in a function rather than a constant. The essence of the diffusion approximation consists of approximating $Q(t)$ by a diffusion process. Under this approximation, the equilibrium number of jobs in the system is found to be geometrically distributed; denoting the state probabilities by p_k, the request arrival rate by λ, and the service time by $\bar{X}$, we have

$$p_k = \begin{cases} 1 - \rho & k = 0 \\ \rho(1 - \hat{\rho})\hat{\rho}^{k-1} & k \geqslant 1, \end{cases} \tag{10.2.1}$$

where, as before, $\rho = \lambda \bar{X}$, and

$$\hat{\rho} = \exp\{-2(1 - \rho)/[\rho C_1^2 + C_2^2]\};$$

the quantities C_1 and C_2 are respectively the coefficients of variation of the inter-arrival and service times, and that these quantities are not both deterministic. Likewise the equilibrium waiting time is found to be exponentially distributed; denoting its probability density function by $f(w)$, we have

$$f(w) = \alpha \exp(-\alpha w), \qquad w \geqslant 0, \tag{10.2.2}$$

where

$$\alpha = 2(1 - \rho)/[\lambda \overline{X^2}], \tag{10.2.3}$$

so that the mean waiting time $1/\alpha$ is in agreement with the Pollaczek–Khintchine formula when specialized to the M/G/1 system. These approximations are valid for $\rho < 1$ and are particularly good for high server utilization.

Example 10.1   Consider a G/G/1 system having an arrival rate of 10 jobs per second, a mean service time of 90 ms, a service time coefficient of variation of 0.5, and an inter-arrival time coefficient of variation of 0.7. Determine the approximate probability that there are two or more jobs in the system during system equilibrium. What is the approximate average waiting time? What are the probabilities that the waiting time exceeds (a) 1 second, and (b) 0.1 second?

Solution Here $\rho = 0.9$, which is near 1, so that the diffusion approximation should be acceptable. The quantity $\hat{\rho}$ is

$$\exp\{-0.2/[0.9 \times 0.49 + 0.25]\} = 0.75. \tag{10.2.2}$$

The probability of having an idle system is 0.1 and that of having exactly one job in the system is $p_1 = 0.9 \times 0.25 = 0.23$. Thus the probability of having two or more jobs in the system is $1 - 0.1 - 0.23 = 0.67$. The second moment of the service time is $0.09^2 \times (1 + 0.5^2) = 0.01$, giving $\alpha = 2 \times 0.1/0.1 = 2$. Thus the mean waiting time is $1/2 = 0.5$ second; the probability that it exceeds 1 second is $\exp(-2) = 0.14$, and the probability that it exceeds 0.1 second is $\exp(-0.2) = 0.82$. □

10.3 Time-Dependent Behaviour of G/G/1

The time-dependent behaviour of the $G/G/1$ system is also based on the diffusion approximation. Denoting the time-dependent cumulative distribution function of the waiting time after the system has been in operation for t units of time by $F(w, t)$, then the diffusion approximation yields

$$F(w, t) = N([w + (1 - \rho)t]/[\lambda \overline{X^2}\sqrt{t}]) - e^{-\alpha w}N([-w + (1 - \rho)t]/[\lambda \overline{X^2}\sqrt{t}]),$$

where α is given by (10.2.3), and $N(.)$ denotes the cumulative distribution function of the standard normal random variable (with zero mean and unit variance), whose values are tabulated in standard statistical tables. This particular approximation holds for all values of ρ (including $\rho > 1$) and is particularly good for high server utilization.

Example 10.2 For the system in the previous example, determine the probability that the waiting time is less than 0.1 second when the system has been in operation for (a) 1 second and (b) 100 seconds.

Solution For (a) the answer is given by

$$F(0.1, 1) = N([0.1 + 0.1]/0.1) - 0.82N(0) = N(2) - 0.82N(0);$$

since the percentage point of the normal distribution $N(2)$ is 0.98, and that for $N(0)$ is 0.5, $F(0.1, 1) = 0.98 - 0.41 = 0.57$. For (b), the corresponding quantity is given by $F(0.1, 100) = N([0.1 + 10]/1.0) - 0.82N([-0.1 + 10]/1.0) = N(10.1) - 0.82N(9.9)$. Now the percentage points of $N(10.1)$ and $N(9.9)$ are both unity, giving $F(0.1, 100) = 1 - 0.82 = 0.18$. This is in agreement with the result in the previous example. □

Example 10.3 For $p > 1$, discuss the behaviour of the waiting time cumulative distribution function $F(w, t)$ as $t \to \infty$.

Solution As $t \to \infty$, the arguments of $N(.)$ evidently also go to infinity, so that the normal cumulative distribution function, when evaluated at these points, are unity. Thus, we conclude that $F(w, \infty) = 1 - \exp(-\alpha w)$, which is in agreement with (10.2.2). □

10.4 Heavy Traffic Approximation for the G/G/m System

An approximation formula is also available for the $G/G/m$ system which is based on the so-called heavy traffic approximation. This approximation is thus particularly good when the system is close to saturation. Using the same notation as in previous sections of this chapter, this approximation states that the waiting time of the $G/G/m$ system is exponentially distributed with mean value

$$\lambda[(C_1/\lambda)^2 + (\bar{X}C_2/m)^2]/[2(1 - \rho)].$$

The stability condition for this system is $\rho = \lambda\bar{X}/m < 1$.

Example 10.4 Consider a $G/G/12$ system with an input rate of 5/second, an average service time of 2 seconds, and with coefficients of variations of the service time and inter-arrival time of respectively 0.8 and 1.4. Estimate the probability that the waiting time is less than 5 seconds.

Solution The mean waiting time for the system in question is

$$5[(1.4/5)^2 + (2 \times 0.8/12)^2]/[2(1 - 10/12)] = 1.44.$$

Thus the required probability is $1 - \exp(-5/1.44) = 0.97$. ▽

10.5 Summary

In this chapter, we have looked at some formulae which are able to convey useful information on the behaviour of systems that are not amenable to exact analysis. We have introduced approximations for the $G/G/1$ system operating under both equilibrium and time-dependent conditions: the equilibrium distribution of the queue size is geometric while that of the waiting time is exponential; the time-dependent behaviour of the waiting time is expressed as a combination of normal distributions. We have also presented an equilibrium approximation to the waiting time of the $G/G/m$ system; it too is expressible in terms of the exponential distribution. Although these formulae do not provide an exact description of the underlying situation, they are nevertheless able to provide meaningful estimates of system behaviour at a fraction of the computational cost, particularly in comparison with a simulation approach which is invariably computation intensive.

10.6 Exercises

1. Consider an $M/M/1$ system with an arrival rate of 10/second, and a service rate of 15/second. Assuming the system is operating in equilibrium,

discuss the accuracy of the diffusion approximation in this situation. What if the arrival rate is reduced to 5/second?

2. Consider a G/G/1 system having an arrival rate of 7 jobs per second, a mean service time of 80 ms, a service time coefficient of variation of 0.4, and an inter-arrival time coefficient of variation of 0.75. Determine the approximate average waiting time and average queue size.

3. Consider a G/M/1 system with an arrival rate of 12/second, and a service rate of 15/second. Discuss how long will it take the system to reach equilibrium, assuming the validity of the diffusion approximation.

4. Consider a G/G/7 system with an input rate of 5/second, an average service time of 1 second, and with coefficients of variations of the service time and inter-arrival time respectively 0.6 and 1.2. Estimate the probability that the waiting time is between 2 and 5 seconds.

5. Consider a M/M/6 system with an input rate of 5/second, an average service time of 1.1 seconds, and with coefficients of variations of the service time and inter-arrival time both of 0.75. Estimate the probability that the waiting time is over 10 seconds.

CHAPTER 11

Workload Modelling and Characterization

11.1 Introduction

In the earlier chapters, mathematical models of complex systems were formulated to analyze system performance. These models are especially useful for prediction and tuning purposes but their applicability to given situations inevitably hinges on the validity of the set of assumptions (e.g. Poisson input) accompanying the analysis. In these analyses, one would often find it difficult to accept the verdict of the analysis without first accepting the underlying model assumptions, which may or may not hold in a given situation.

In contrast to analytic modelling, which was the principal focus in previous chapters, *performance measurement* is essentially empirical in character and is chiefly concerned with the behaviour of systems which already exist in some form. In performance measurement, one is often interested in the workload presented to the system, and by suitably feeding a representative load into an actual system, the latter's performance may be measured. There is no doubt that the performance of a system critically depends on its workload, and performance may be unsatisfactory or satisfactory according to whether the work demanded of it is excessive or not.

In ascertaining the performance of an actual system, it is frequently impractical to carry out detailed measurements of the entire production workload involved because of the resources required. For instance, before replacing an existing system by a new one, it is often necessary to perform actual tests on the target configuration (for example, at the manufacturer's site). In such a situation, it is not possible to transfer the entire production workload to the manufacturer's site for evaluation, since running the full workload may require weeks or even months of machine time. Therefore, one often needs to extract a *representative workload* of the installation for meaningful evaluation. The term *workload model* is often employed to signify programs used to represent the workload of an installation; it can be a sample of the actual programs of the workload of the installation or synthetic programs specially designed and created to model the workload. The set of programs in a workload model however, is generally not the same as the full workload itself. A workload model, therefore, may be viewed as a kind of averaging operation on the underlying workload, and should provide a representative characterization of the full workload being modelled. Workload models may be distinguished into *executable* and *nonexecutable* models. An executable workload model corresponds to programs which are executable on the system being evaluated; through the actual running of these programs on the target system, the latter's performance may be directly measured. A nonexecutable workload model, on the other hand, is not used to drive a real system but is employed to derive performance characteristics either by analytic calculation or by simulation.

11.2 Benchmarks

Benchmarks are a sample of actual jobs considered to be representative of the entire workload. Benchmarks are executable workload models and allow different machine components (e.g. CPU, memory, I/O) as well as different software tasks (e.g. compilation, sorting) to be evaluated. Among the criteria which may be used for benchmark selection are: jobs most frequently run, jobs taking up most of the machine processing time and critical jobs.

One problem with benchmarks is that of *scaling*: in order to have an accurate representation of the associated workload, a large number of jobs may need to be included whose total run time may be prohibitive for evaluation purposes. A second problem with benchmarks is their inherent *inflexibility*: it is often difficult to modify benchmarks in order to increase their representativeness. It is, however, possible to introduce relatively crude modifications such as the suppression of certain job steps and the suppression of output generation. A third problem with benchmarks is that jobs suitable for incorporation may not be included for security reasons; real data files, too, may not be available to support the evaluation as they may contain sensitive and confidential information.

11.3 Synthetic Jobs

An evaluation method which overcomes the scaling problem present in benchmarks is to make use of synthetic jobs. These jobs are not existing jobs but are artificially constructed to reflect the actual workload characteristics. Like benchmarks, they are executable workload models and may be used to test different components and tasks in the system. Synthetic jobs are often parameterized so that by suitably adjusting a number of input parameters, they may be made to produce different patterns of behaviour. For example, parameters may represent the number of disk blocks transferred, or the number of times a given computation loop is executed.

The key advantage of synthetic jobs is its flexibility. Flexibility could be introduced through the initial design of the overall program structure, as well as through the use of parameters. Such flexibility may be exploited to evaluate system behaviour under extreme conditions which may represent a projected future situation or one occurring infrequently. This kind of evaluation is generally not possible with benchmarks. However, the use of synthetic jobs has its disadvantages: their construction, particularly the design of a suitable

126

and sufficiently flexible overall program structure, may be difficult; the adjustments of the parameters in order to faithfully model the actual workload may also be difficult. The overhead of developing the synthetic job—design, coding, debugging and testing—may also be significant. The construction of useful synthetic jobs generally necessitates a careful analysis of existing workload.

11.4 Kernels

Very often, in order to compare the performance of different machines in a uniform manner, standardized programs, called *kernels*, are used. Kernels are executable workload models in which both relatively simple computation and elaborate data processing may be represented; kernel programs may range from specialized mathematical routines such as matrix inversion and polynomial evaluation, to full-scale application systems such as payroll and order processing. Typical kernels may include tasks such as file processing, sorting, and mathematical computation.

To provide flexibility, kernels may be made to be parameter driven like synthetic programs. In most cases, especially when elaborate processing is involved, performance is assessed by measuring the time required to actually run the kernel. In simple cases, however, it may be possible to calculate the processing time of a particular kernel from the manufacturer's instruction timings without running it; to do this it is often necessary to reduce the kernel to a set of elementary instructions. In the context of machine selection and performance comparison, kernels are sometimes also referred to as *standardized benchmarks*. Unlike simple instruction mixes (see below), kernels tend to be oriented to specific processing tasks; thus, as far as these specific tasks are concerned, they usually provide a more meaningful evaluation of performance than instruction mixes.

11.5 Scripts

In interactive systems, workloads are generated by terminal users who follow scripts of commands. A *script* is a sequence of interactive commands interspersed with think times. In order to ascertain the performance of an interactive system, it is often necessary to have a large number of simultaneous interactive users, each generating workload for the system through the use of typical scripts. Scripts are executable workload models. A typical script may involve the following activities:

- login
- check mail (this may involve reading new messages as well as stepping through some of the older ones)
- answer and send new messages (this typically involves entering message text and some editing)

- type in a source program
- compile the program
- edit the program to remove errors
- re-compile program
- run the program
- debug the program (this will involve further editing)
- re-compile program
- run the program
- list the program and associated files on line printer
- rename program
- logout.

By the judicious use of an assortment of typical scripts, the workload of an interactive system may be meaningfully represented, and its performance behaviour may be ascertained by observation and measurement.

Example 11.1 In an office environment, the principal function of the computer system is concerned with message communications among office workers. Provide a possible script for this situation.

Solution. Here the tasks of program compilation and execution are not carried out. Since message communication is the main task, it is possible that the printing and filing of messages may be a common activity. The following is a possible script for this working environment:

- login
- check mail
- answer and send new messages
- print message
- file message
- logout. □

11.6 Instruction Mixes

System workload may be regarded as being made up of a series of instructions of various types. A particular workload is characterized by how often the different types of instructions are used. Thus, by suitably mixing the instructions in the right proportion, a workload model may be obtained. An instruction mix model is nonexecutable and is primarily geared to the evaluation of CPU performance; the key parameters used are the relative frequencies of the instructions and their corresponding execution times. If there are n instruction types with relative usage frequencies p_i, $i = 1, \ldots, n$ with

128

Table 11.1 A possible instruction
classification

1.	Load/store
2.	Fixed point add/subtract
3.	Fixed point multiply/divide
4.	Floating point add/subtract
5.	Floating point multiply/divide
6.	Logical
7.	Branch
8.	Compare
9.	Shifts
10.	Miscellaneous

$p_1 + \ldots + p_n = 1$, and if their corresponding execution times are t_i, $i = 1, \ldots, n$, then from these one may calculate the average instruction time T,

$$T = \sum_{i=1}^{n} p_i t_i. \tag{11.6.1}$$

By determining this average for different systems, one can have a meaningful comparison of performance. Here, what characterizes the workload is the sequence $\{p_i\}$ and different values for this sequence result in a different mix. The sequence $\{t_i\}$, on the other hand, represents the characteristics of a given system, and different systems have different values for this sequence. In the older machines, the instruction set tends to be large, and the instructions tend to be rather complex. In the recent reduced instruction set computers (RISCs), however, the instruction set tends to be smaller and the machine instructions tend to be simpler, which generally permit them to execute in one cycle; for RISCs, all the t_i are the same and equal to one machine cycle, and T can thus be obtained on the basis of the usage frequencies alone.

In an instruction mix model, it is often not advisable to model the workload using instructions of too elementary a nature as such a representation is invariably highly system-dependent: elementary instructions present in one system may have no equivalence in another one, and this makes direct comparison difficult. It is often useful instead to group instructions into wider classes which are found in most systems so as to facilitate direct comparison; in the course of such grouping, additional averaging of instruction times within classes is required. An example of such classification is given in Table 11.1.

While the sequence of timings $\{t_i\}$ may be obtained from the manufacturers, the sequence $\{p_i\}$ which represents the workload characteristics must be estimated or measured. These estimates may be formed from data obtained from, for example, a software monitor (described in the next chapter). Alternatively, one may use standard mixes which are applicable to a particular processing environment, which are compiled from data gathered from a large

Table 11.2

Instructions	Relative frequency (%)
1. Load/store	31.2
2. Index	18.0
3. Branch	16.6
4. Compare	3.8
5. Fixed point	6.9
6. Floating point	12.2
7. Shift/logical	6.0
8. Miscellaneous	5.3

number of similar installations. For example, a common standard mix (Flynn 1974)) for a scientific environment is given in Table 11.2.

Example 11.2 An installation which is mostly concerned with scientific applications is considering upgrading its machine. The average instruction time for its current machine is found to be 4.5 μs. It is considered that the replacement machine should at least be twice as fast as the present one. The instruction timings information available for a particular new machine (in microseconds) is

Load/store	2.0
Fixed point	1.8
Floating point	4.3
Shift/logical	1.4
Others	1.7

Using the mix given in Table 11.2 as a guide, determine whether this machine is worthy of further consideration.

Solution. Applying equation (11.6.1) and using the relative frequencies given in Table 11.2, we obtain from the timings information given $T = 2.1 \mu$s. We have assumed that instructions not explicitly mentioned takes 1.7 μs to execute.) Since this is less than half of 4.5 μs, this particular new machine is therefore worthy of further consideration according to the given criterion. ∇

1.7 Measure of Computing Power

An instruction mix model suffers from the drawback that it takes into account only instruction execution time and fails to take into account other factors such as memory size, word length, and I/O speed, which also have an important bearing on performance. A measure of computing power proposed by Knight (1968), which incorporates these factors is

$$P = \frac{10^{12}[(L - 7)\, MW/K]^i}{T_{cpu} + T_{I/O}},$$

(11.7.1)

where

L = word length in bits,
M = memory size in words,
K = 928 000
T_{cpu} = average time in microseconds for the CPU to perform one million operations and equals 10^6 multiplied by the quantity T given in (11.6.1),
$T_{I/O}$ = nonoverlapped I/O time in microseconds for one million I/O operations (this is dependent on factors such as the channel width, transfer rate etc.)

W is the word factor and = $\begin{cases} 1 \text{ for fixed-word-length memory} \\ 2 \text{ for variable-word-length memory} \end{cases}$

i is the exponential memory weighting factor and = $\begin{cases} \frac{1}{2} \text{ for scientific computation} \\ \frac{1}{3} \text{ for commercial computation.} \end{cases}$

Example 11.3. Consider a machine with fixed word length and a memory size of $M = 1$ million words. Determine how the word lengths of 16 bits and 32 bits affect the computing power available for (a) scientific applications, and (b) commercial applications, assuming all other factors being equal.

Solution. For $L = 16$, the ratio of the computing power available for scientific computation to that available for commercial computation, from formula (11.7.1), is 1.46, which means that there is about 46% more computing power available for scientific computations. Likewise, for $L = 32$, the corresponding ratio is 1.71, which means that there is about 71% more computing power available for scientific computations. $\square$

11.8 Summary

In this chapter, a number of approaches were introduced to model and characterize given workloads so as to facilitate a meaningful assessment of performance. Benchmarks are a selection of existing jobs considered to be representative of the full workload being modelled, while synthetic jobs are ones artificially created to reflect the characteristics of the workload. Kernels are standardized programs which facilitate the direct comparison of different systems in a uniform manner. Scripts aim to model the behaviour of typical terminal users to determine the workload in an interactive system. Instruction

Table 11.3

	CPU I	*CPU II*
Move	0.4	0.7
Fixed point	0.4	0.5
Branch	0.6	0.8
Load	0.7	0.4

mixes consist of calculating the average instruction execution time appropriately weighted, the weighting factor being determined by the characteristics of the workload. The measure of computing power may be regarded as a refinement of the instruction mix method with factors other than the instruction execution time, such as the memory size, I/O speed, taken into consideration.

11.9 Exercises

1. Explain the main problems associated with benchmarks selection. Discuss why selection on the basis of jobs most frequently run may give unreliable results. How do benchmarks compare with synthetic programs?

2. Consider Table 11.2, given in Example 11.2. Suppose the load/store operation is slowed down by a factor of 2. Determine how much faster floating point operations must be performed in order to give the same level of performance, assuming all other instruction timings are unchanged.

3. A particular algorithm requires the following instructions to be executed with the given relative frequencies (%):

Move	30	Branch	8
Fixed point	12	Load	50

Compare the performance in executing this algorithm of two CPUs with respective instruction timings in microseconds given in Table 11.3.

4. Consider a machine with fixed length memory. Discuss how the size of the memory affects the computing power available for (a) scientific applications, and (b) commercial applications, assuming all other factors are equal.

CHAPTER 12

Performance Measurement and Monitoring

12.1 Introduction

For a variety of reasons, it is often necessary to gather information on the performance of an existing system. Some of the reasons for doing so are: to detect any potential or actual performance problems; to determine the job behaviour of the installation (e.g. whether most jobs are I/O bound or CPU bound); to determine the workload characteristics (e.g. the frequency that given instructions are executed); to tune the existing system to improve performance. Performance monitoring consists of gathering data on the performance of an existing system during its operation, and the subsequent reduction of the data collected to a form suitable for interpretation. The collection of data often takes the form of either *counting* the occurrence of certain events, or the more detailed *tracing* of event sequences which records the development of related series of events and the times of their occurrence. In order to carry out measurement on a system, one needs to have specialized measuring equipments and tools. Measuring a system almost invariably produces *interference* to its normal behaviour and consequently introduces error into the measurement; in some cases such errors may be excessive but in other cases they may be insignificant or suitably filtered out. Monitoring tools may fall into one of four categories: hardware monitor, software monitor, firmware monitor, and hybrid monitor.

12.2 Hardware Monitors

A hardware monitor is a tool for measuring electrical events in a computer. Normally hardware monitors are devices external to the computer being monitored (the host computer) but sometimes could be built into the host computer in certain circumstances. A hardware monitor could be itself a computer. A hardware monitor makes use of a set of probes for signal detection which are so designed that they cause minimum interference to the host system. These probes are connected to the appropriate points in the host systems whose activities are being monitored. The signals from the probes are passed through *logical filter circuits* which allow signals from different probes to be logically combined to yield events of interest. For example, by sensing

132

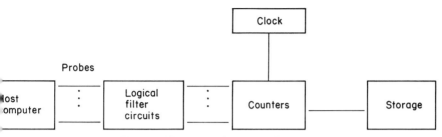

FIGURE 12.1.   Hardware monitor

CHANNEL BUSY with one probe and CPU BUSY with another, one can detect the times when the channel is busy while the CPU is idle using the logical functions AND and NOT. If it is discovered that the CPU is mostly idle whenever the channel is busy, then this may signify that there is very little CPU/channel overlap and the CPU may be spending an excessive amount of time in waiting for I/O. Occurrence of events are counted by means of *counters* in the hardware monitor, which are also able to measure the time interval between events by counting the number of intervening clock pulses. Thus, apart from receiving input from the logical filter, the counter also receives input from the clock. A diagrammatic representation of a hardware monitor is shown in Fig. 12.1. The counter contents may be displayed visually but more often are periodically transferred to storage (typically magnetic tapes) for later processing; such processing may involve data reduction, statistical analysis, data interpretation, and report generation.

Since events in a computer system occur at very high speed, it is essential that a hardware monitor has the required *resolution*; i.e. it must be able to sample events at a sufficiently high frequency so that events are not missed due to the failure of the monitor's sampling rate to match that of event occurrences in the host computer. Examples of performance behaviour which may be revealed or ascertained by hardware monitoring are: channel load balancing—whether one channel is overloaded and another is poorly utilized; CPU and I/O overlap—too little overlap may indicate the presence of a problem; excessive disk contention—whether a particular disk is sustaining most of the activity (if this is the case, it may signify a poor spread of files across disk modules).

It must be pointed out that while hardware monitors are able to point to problem spots, they generally do not provide sufficiently detailed information on the cause of the problems and how these problems could be tackled. A software monitor, on the other hand, is normally able to furnish more detailed information than a hardware monitor.

12.3   Software Monitors

As indicated above, a hardware monitor is merely able to point to trouble spots in the system when the smooth flow of work is checked as a result of overloading, device contention and the presence of bottlenecks. In order to solve the performance problems revealed by a hardware monitor, more detailed information is required, and such information may be gathered by means of a software monitor. Software monitors are programs used for the purpose of collecting performance information, and are invoked at appropriate times depending on whether the monitor is an *event-driven* monitor or a *sample-driven* monitor. In addition to the common performance measures such as device utilization, throughput, response time, and queue length, a software monitor is also able to measure process characteristics such as the execution frequency of specific instruction types, the rate of specific interrupt types, and how often a particular variable or data structure is accessed. The data which can be collected by a software monitor are those related to the software level; electrical signals such as voltage levels or pulses cannot in general be detected.

In an event-driven software monitor, the gathering of performance data is triggered off by particular events, typically the execution of specific instructions. The execution of specific instructions may be detected by the insertion of a *software probe* whereby normal processing is interrupted and the monitor is invoked whenever the monitored instructions are executed. The invocation of the monitor has the effect of recording relevant details relating to the execution of the monitored instructions such as the updating of a register and the use of specified memory locations. Software probes may be inserted into an application program or a system program depending on whether interest is focused on particular applications or the system. A sample-driven software monitor, on the other hand, gathers data at prespecified time intervals, which may be fixed or variable, deterministic or random.

In its simplest form, software monitors may be little different from job accounting routines which gather statistics for charging purposes. Since charging algorithms are often based on information such as CPU time, disk usage, and memory residence time, job accounting routines are frequently able to provide a rich source of relevant performance information. However, such information is chiefly geared to accounting rather than performance assessment, and interests are focused on statistics relating to individual applications rather than those of the system as a whole.

Since software monitors require extra instructions to be executed, they produce interference in several respects:

- *Memory space interference.* This is caused by storing the extra instructions as well as the data collected in memory.

- *Execution time interference.* This is caused by the extra time required to fetch, decode and execute the extra instructions.

- *Interrupt interference.* During the execution of the extra instructions, certain interrupts may be disabled; this will adversely affect the system's response to processes which give rise to the disabled interrupts.

Table 12.1

	% of time in problem program state	% of time in supervisor state	% of time busy
Software monitor	49	9	58
Hardware monitor	35	30	65

Thus during a monitoring session, the utilizations of both memory and CPU are higher than they are otherwise. Interrupt problems may also yield biased data as it may not be possible for certain critical processes to be interrupted by the monitor so that samples relating to these situations are not collected; for example, if CPU utilization statistics is being gathered, then the inability of the monitor to interrupt will cause samples which otherwise record a CPU BUSY condition to be lost.

Compared with hardware monitors, software monitors generally have lower resolution and higher interference, so that data collected by the former is generally more accurate. On the other hand, software monitors, being programs, are much more flexible and have a wider scope than hardware programs, are much more flexible than hardware monitors. Unlike hardware monitors, software monitors need to interact closely with the host operating system so that, as measurement tools, they are generally not very portable.

Example 12.1   The results in Table 12.1 are obtained from measuring the CPU activity of a system using a sample-driven software monitor, and a hardware monitor under identical workload conditions. Give a possible explanation of the discrepancy in the measurements.

Solution.   Taking a sample in software monitoring will involve interrupting the CPU. Unlike in the problem program state, a CPU in the supervisor state is not always interruptible, as certain low priority interrupts are disabled in that state. Thus when a sampling epoch finds the CPU in the supervisor state, it may not actually be allowed to proceed with the sampling, so that the fact that the CPU is observed in the supervisor state is not recorded. Accordingly this will result in a lower reading for the second column and a correspondingly higher reading for the first column in the above table.   □

12.4   Firmware and Hybrid Monitors

Microprograms represent a layer of programming below the machine language level in a computer, and they reside in a store, the *control store*, which is normally several times faster than main memory. In some systems, the entire

136

machine language instruction set is implemented by microprograms with each instruction corresponding to a specific microprogram. The firmware of the computer refers to the collection of microprograms in its control store, and a firmware monitor may be viewed as a software monitor with the difference that the extra monitoring instructions are implemented as microprograms. Since the control store is much faster than main memory, firmware monitors are able to reduce time interference through reducing instruction fetch times. However, since the size of control stores is much smaller than that of main memory, microprograms are generally less versatile than normal programs; accordingly the types and details of data collected from firmware monitors are somewhat limited in scope compared with software monitors, but they do offer a significant degree of versatility and flexibility over those of a hardware monitor. Not infrequently, software monitors are supplemented by firmware additions to the host system to aid the monitoring task.

A *hybrid monitor* consists of a hardware monitor complemented by a software or firmware monitor. This cooperation augments the versatility of the hardware monitor and allows more detailed information on the cause of certain events to be obtained. On the other hand, the hardware monitor can relieve the software monitor of some of the latter's tasks such as data recording and reduction; in this way the interference caused to the host system by the software monitor may be reduced.

12.5 Presentation and Interpretation of Measurement Results

The data collected from measurement experiments are often considerable, and the mass of raw data in unprocessed form is of limited value. It is through suitably transforming and summarizing them that they become meaningful and usable. A clear and concise presentation of measurement results will facilitate the correct diagnosis of any performance problems, and permit the correct remedial actions to be identified.

In Chapter 2, some general techniques (such as histograms, averages) for displaying and summarizing vast amounts of data to facilitate their interpretation have been discussed. They are undoubtedly also applicable to the processing of measurement data; however, in this section, we shall describe two common schemes which are specifically geared to the presentation of computer performance measurements; they are (1) Gantt charts, and (2) Kiviat graphs.

12.5.1 *Gantt Charts*

The *system utilisation profile* gives information on the utilization patterns of the major resources of the system together with any relevant overlap information. A *Gantt chart* consists of a number of suitably labelled horizontal lines; each line corresponds to a given system state with the length of the line signifying the relative proportion of time that the system spends in that state.

Table 12.2

System state	Utilization (%)
CPU busy	57
CPU and channel overlap	25
CPU in problem program state	48
Any channel busy	58

By comparing the relative magnitudes of different lines, a pattern of overall system efficiency may be obtained. Representation of system profile by means of a Gantt chart allows the salient performance features of the system to be captured at a glance.

Example 12.2 From the basic numerical system profile obtained from a measurement experiment given in Table 12.2, expand the table to include the following quantities:

CPU only
CPU in supervisor state
channel only
system idle.

Hence provide a Gantt chart representation of the system utilization profile.

Solution. The required quantities may be derived from those given in the table as follows.

CPU only = CPU busy − CPU and channel overlap = 32%
CPU in supervisor state = CPU busy − CPU in problem program state = 9%
channel only = Any channel busy − CPU and channel overlap = 33%
system idle = 1 − CPU only − channel only − CPU and channel overlap = 10%

The expanded table is given as Table 12.3.
A Gantt chart representation of these utilization figures is shown in Fig. 12.2. □

12.5.2 Kiviat Graphs

Although a Gantt chart provides a useful summary and display of the key resource utilization characteristics, it does not enable one to tell quickly whether the system in fact behaves in an efficient and satisfactory manner. By suitably representing the information in a Kiviat graph, it is often possible to

Table 12.3

System state	Utilization (%)
CPU busy	57
CPU and channel overlap	25
CPU in problem program state	48
Any channel busy	58
CPU only	32
CPU in supervisor state	9
Channel only	33
System idle	10

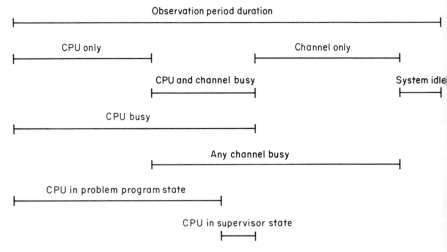

FIGURE 12.2.   A Gantt chart

quickly recognize whether the system profile represents a desirable state of affairs.

A *Kiviat graph* exhibits a circular pattern with a number of radial axes used to plot the utilizations of various system states. A key feature of a Kiviat graph—one which facilitates meaningful interpretation—is that the axes are so chosen that states which take on high utilization values when the system is performing well are alternated with those taking on small values when the system is performing well. This convention permits performance patterns to be recognized quickly so that for optimal performance, the corresponding Kiviat graph should exhibit a sharply defined star shape. Fig. 12.3 shows an example of a Kiviat graph corresponding to an efficient, well-balanced system. Thus by perceiving how much a given Kiviat graph deviates from an ideal star

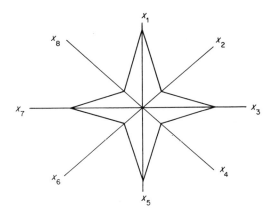

x_1 = CPU busy
x_2 = CPU only
x_3 = CPU and channel overlap
x_4 = Channel only
x_5 = Any channel busy
x_6 = CPU idle
x_7 = CPU in problem program state
x_8 = CPU in supervisor state

FIGURE 12.3.   A Kiviat graph

shape, one could have an intuitive feel as to whether a system is performing satisfactorily, and if not, what are the potential problems.

Example 12.3   Construct a Kiviat graph from the data given in the Table 12.4; comment on whether the system is performing satisfactorily and identify any potential performance problems.

Solution.   The required Kiviat graph is shown in Fig. 12.4. We see that it departs considerably from the ideal star shape. In particular, there is not sufficient overlap between I/O and CPU, which means it is possible that the CPU may be spending a considerable amount of time waiting for the completion of I/O operations in order to process the data obtained. It also shows that the CPU is spending a substantial amount of time in the supervisor state, which suggests that a fair proportion of the CPU cycles are used by the CPU in 'thinking' (i.e. organizing its own work) rather than solving the users' problems. The overall performance behaviour of the system is therefore unsatisfactory.   □

140

Table 12.4

System state	Utilization (%)
CPU busy	57
CPU and channel overlap	11
CPU in problem program state	30
Any channel busy	53
CPU only	46
CPU in supervisor state	27
Channel only	42

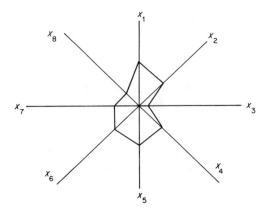

x_1 = CPU busy

x_2 = CPU only

x_3 = CPU and channel overlap

x_4 = Channel only

x_5 = Any channel busy

x_6 = CPU idle

x_7 = CPU in problem program state

x_8 = CPU in supervisor state

FIGURE 12.4.   A Kiviat graph of Example 12.3

Table 12.5

System state	Utilization (%)
CPU busy	20
CPU and channel overlap	25
CPU in problem program state	15
Any channel busy	74

12.6 Summary

Collecting performance data from a computer system could be effected by a hardware monitor, a software monitor, a firmware monitor, or a suitable combination of these. The nature of the measured data may be related to a count of the occurrence of certain events, or to the tracing of certain event sequences. Obtaining information about a system through measurement almost always introduces some interference to its usual behaviour, so that there are often measurement errors.

Monitors are generally able to accumulate vast amounts of data; the suitable reduction and presentation of data therefore constitutes an important, integral aspect of measurement experimentation. Two common methods for data presentation have been described—Gantt charts and Kiviat graphs—both of which are able to provide a meaningful summary of overall system behaviour. The latter, in particular, facilitates judgements to be made concerning the satisfactoriness of a given system and helps to identify possible performance problems.

12.7 Exercises

1. What are the main features of a hardware monitor? Discuss the principal disadvantages of the hardware monitor.

2. Assess the relative merits of hardware and software monitors in performance measurement. Discuss the extent to which software monitors can give unreliable results.

3. From the measurements given in Table 12.5, derive the following quantities: CPU only, CPU in supervisor state, channel only, system idle. Hence provide a Gantt chart representation of the system utilization profile.

4. From the quantities given in the previous exercise, suggest a set of axes suitable for producing a Kiviat graph. Hence, produce a Kiviat graph using the numerical values provided there.

5. What are the main decisions involved in producing (a) Gantt charts, and (b) Kiviat graphs? Compare the relative merits of Gantt charts and Kiviat graphs with respect to the representation and interpretation of measurement data.

CHAPTER 13

Performance Tuning and Improvement

13.1 Introduction

Measurement and monitoring allows the detection of performance trouble spots and helps to diagnose the cause of these problems. Frequently, knowing what went wrong in a system does not immediately suggest a suitable cure partly because of the limited courses of action available and partly because of external constraints. For example, if it is observed that particular components of the system are responding too slowly, then an obvious solution may be to simply upgrade them to faster ones; however, when one has to work within a given budget constraint, this may not be the best or even an acceptable course of action. In this chapter, we shall examine some of the common performance problems and suggest possible ways of overcoming them without increasing the level of available resources. We are primarily interested in 'software' rather than 'hardware' solutions in that we aim to introduce improvement in existing systems so as to bring out the performance potential in them without altering their hardware characteristics.

13.2 General System Tuning

A common performance problem is *resource contention*, which may be associated with devices such as disks or channels. Apart from the obvious solution of making the devices in question faster through upgrading, it may be possible to reduce contention by a redistribution of load over similar devices. In the case of disks, excessive contention for a particular drive may be relieved by transferring some of the files responsible for an appreciable volume of I/O activities to another drive. Where there are similar devices with differing operating speeds, suitably balancing the load among the devices will almost certainly be beneficial. A quantitative assessment and possible guidelines for load balancing and optimization are examined in detail in Section 13.4. In certain devices, it is possible to reduce the device service time, which has the effect of decreasing overall loading on the device. In the case of channel contention, the use of rotational position sensing (see Chapter 2)—i.e. limiting the channel connection time to instants when data transfer can actually take place rather than having the channel tied up throughout the entire latency period—will reduce overall channel loading. More precisely, suppose the input traffic to a channel is λ requests per second, and the time required for one revolution of the disks served by the channel is T. If the average time required to transfer a block of data through the channel is $\bar{\tau}$, then since the rotational delay incurred prior to data transfer is half a disc revolution on average, the reduction in channel traffic intensity due to the adoption of rotational position sensing is consequently

$$\lambda(T/2 + \bar{\tau}) - \lambda\bar{\tau} = \lambda T/2.$$

Under severe contention, λ is likely to be large so that the reduction in loading of $\lambda T/2$ will be particularly significant. In the case of the moving head disk, too, it is often possible to reduce seek time by judicious data placement. A more detailed examination of seek time reduction may be found in Chapter 9.

Poor CPU and I/O overlap is another common performance problem, which may signify an imbalance demand for resources among the jobs scheduled to run concurrently. If this is the cause, then suitable alterations to the production job schedule may improve overlap. *Low resource utilization* may also be undesirable since it indicates that the full processing potential cannot be realized, and it may mean that many of the resources are often in an idle state waiting for work; this situation may be possibly remedied through stepping up the degree of multiprogramming by having more concurrent jobs.

If the system is found to spend a *large proportion of time in the supervisor mode*, then this means that the operation of the system is incurring substantial overheads with the system spending an excessive amount of its time engaged in 'thinking'—i.e. organizing its own work—rather than doing useful work for the users. This may be caused by an inordinate degree of multiprogramming and/or the execution of highly complex system scheduling algorithms. In such a situation, lowering the level of job concurrency and simplifying these scheduling algorithms may lead to improvement.

In a virtual storage system, sometimes too much I/O traffic may be the result of *thrashing*—i.e. excessive page faults are generated due to an over-commitment of real memory. This may indicate a severe competition for main memory among jobs or it may be a consequence of certain highly active system modules being frequently paged out by the page-turning algorithm. One way of improving this situation is to permanently fix these active routines in main memory so that they are not selected by the paging algorithm for replacement; judiciously modifying the page-replacement algorithm may sometimes yield beneficial effects. Lowering the degree of multiprogramming, too, may relief the over-commitment of real memory.

Increasing the degree of multiprogramming has two main effects: a generally beneficial one of increasing resource utilization, and a non-beneficial one of increasing system overhead. Increasing the resource utilization is often desirable but is not always so; it is so only if the increased utilization corresponds to useful work done for the user rather than work done by the system for itself in organizing its own activities. An increase in the system overhead,

144

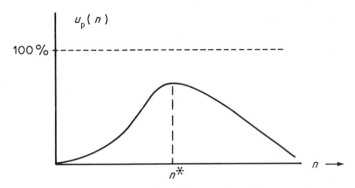

FIGURE 13.1.   The optimal degree of multiprogramming

obviously, is always undesirable. There is an optimal degree of multiprogramming which represents the most efficient balance of these two
opposing effects. For instance, if $u(n)$ signifies the CPU utilization relating to
a multiprogramming level of n, then as long as $u(n) < 1$, it is typically an
increasing function of n. Likewise, if $u_s(n)$ signifies the fraction of time that
the CPU spends in the supervisor mode, which may be viewed as the overhead
in this context, then it too will be an increasing function of the degree of
multiprogramming n, providing $u(n)$ and hence $u_s(n)$ are less than unity; this
is so because when more jobs are being run, there is correspondingly more
organization work involved. If we take the quantity $u_p(n)$, which signifies the
fraction of time that the CPU is spent in the problem program mode under
multiprogramming level n, as our performance index, then evidently

$$u_p(n) = u(n) - u_s(n), \tag{13.2.1}$$

since the CPU, when busy, may be only in either problem program or
supervisor mode. Thus for optimal performance we need to maximize $u_p(n)$
by varying n. Due to the characteristic pattern of increase in the functions
$u(n)$ an $u_s(n)$, the user utilization curve $u_p(n)$ typically exhibits the form as
shown in Fig. 13.1, with n^* representing the optimal degree of multiprogramming. In principle, if the form of the functions $u(n)$ and $u_s(n)$ are
known, then n^* may be determined analytically, for example, by differentiation. In practice, however, these functions can only be determined
empirically since they are unlikely to admit closed-form representations. In
general, determining the optimal operating level n^* in a practical processing
environment can be accomplished by careful and well-planned experimentation. The method of *evolutionary operations* may, for example, be used
to help determine n^*; with this method, different values of n are set for
different operating periods and the value which yields optimal performance

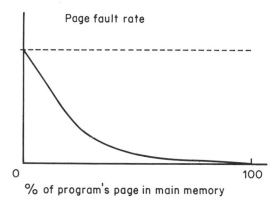

FIGURE 13.2.   Non-uniform character of program referencing behaviour

can be adopted until there is a significant change in workload characteristics, when it will be similarly re-determined. This experimentation scheme can be of considerable value in computer performance tuning and has been applied to the tuning of parameters in dynamic storage management algorithms (Leung (1982b)).

13.3   Program Behaviour and Execution Efficiency

Effective performance management can be achieved only with adequate knowledge of how processes in the system behave. It is empirically found that most program executions exhibit the *locality* property: programs tend to reference storage in a localized, non-uniform manner. Locality referencing may be divided into *spatial locality* and *temporal locality*. The former means that program references are likely to be clustered and concentrated in a small subset of the available memory addresses; as program execution progresses, spatial locality slowly changes. Spatial locality referencing is not unreasonable as program instructions are mostly sequentially executed with related variables tending to be placed close together; most data structures, too, tend to be localized and span a number of consecutive locations in memory. Temporal locality means that during any phase of program execution, memory locations which have been recently referenced are likely to be re-referenced in the near future. Among the possible causes of temporal locality referencing are looping, and the ongoing updating of certain data structures and variables.

   In a paging system, locality referencing means that during any phase of program execution, a program tends to favour a subset of its pages which are often close to each other in the virtual address space, and this set of pages tends to change membership slowly over time. Figure 13.2 illustrates the non-

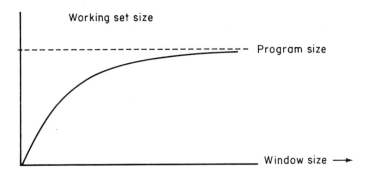

FIGURE 13.3.   Relationship between working set and window sizes

uniform nature of program referencing in a paging system at a particular phase of execution. The y-axis there shows the page fault rate, where a page fault signifies a situation where a page not present in main memory is referenced by the program; it causes the system to fetch the missing page from secondary memory. We see that, beyond a certain point, having more of the program in main memory makes little difference to the execution efficiency of the program. However, when the favoured subset of pages of the program is not all present in main memory, the page fault rate rises very sharply, with a consequential reduction in execution efficiency.

Temporal locality referencing in a paging system suggests that at a particular time t, the most useful pages are in the *working set* $W(t, h)$, which is the set of distinct pages referred to by the program in the time interval $[t - h, t]$, where h is known as the window size. A graph showing the relationship between the working set size and the window size is shown in Figure 13.3. In order to meaningfully define the program locality, a suitable value for the window size h^* must be chosen. Too large a value for h^* may include virtually the whole program, while too small a value for it causes an excessive number of page faults to be generated, leading to possible thrashing.

Once a value of h^* is determined, then an effective strategy for controlling efficiency is to allow a program to be activated when there is enough memory space available to hold its working set $W(t, h^*)$. When there is not enough space to hold $W(t, h^*)$, then it may be advisable to swap out that program, and either concentrate on the remaining concurrent programs or swap one in with a smaller working set.

Another consideration which would affect the execution efficiency of programs is the possibility of system failure. Computer systems are never totally reliable and their unreliability invariably manifests in unexpected failures. Such failures are undesirable as they often give rise to wasted processing, or even sometimes lost information. Wasted processing means that the system is engaged in performing the same work more than once, and this frequently represents a severe erosion of machine resources and system capacity. To combat and soften the effects of unexpected failures, *checkpoints* are often used, whereby when failures do occur, their damage is localized. Avoiding the need for re-processing from the very start, checkpoints limit re-processing from the previous successfully created checkpoint, and any processing performed before that checkpoint need not be repeated. Thus, it would appear that the smaller the inter-checkpoint interval, the smaller is this amount of re-processing. However, checkpointing is accompanied by an appreciable amount of overhead: creating a checkpoint requires additional time; so too is the resumption of normal processing from a checkpoint following a failure. Therefore having an excessive number of checkpoints in a program is undesirable because of the overheads involved; on the other hand, having too few checkpoints means that substantial re-processing is inevitable following a failure. An efficient checkpointing scheme should therefore maintain a suitable balance between these opposing factors; such a scheme substantially improves the efficiency of programs executed in an unreliable system environment. The problem of optimal program checkpointing is beyond the scope of this book; however, a detailed study may be found in Leung and Choo (1984a).

13.4 Load Balancing and Optimization

When there are a number of devices supporting similar processing functions, then a decision is called for to spread the workload among them. In cases where all the devices have the same operating speed and characteristics, then an even spread of the workload among them is an obvious solution. However, when the devices have different processing speeds, then spreading the workload to achieve maximum efficiency requires more detailed consideration. In this section, we shall examine the problem of spreading workload in an optimal manner among devices with different processing speeds.

Suppose there are n devices, with respective mean processing times of $\bar{X}_i$, $i = 1, \ldots, n$, and their aggregate workload is represented by a Poisson process with input request rate λ. The problem is to minimize the mean response time $\bar{R}$ suitably averaged over the different devices, with the weighting factor applied to a given device equal to the proportion of requests directed to it:

$$\bar{R} = \sum_{i=1}^{n} (\lambda_i/\lambda)\, \bar{R}_i,$$

where $\bar{R}_i$ is the mean response time relating to the ith device, and λ_i is the amount of traffic routed to it. For simplicity, we shall concentrate on situations where the individual service times are exponentially distributed; thus we can apply the M/M/1 response time formula in the expansion of $\bar{R}_i$. Our problem

148

is thus reduced to

$$\text{minimize } \bar{R} = \sum_{i=1}^{n} (\lambda_i/\lambda)\, \bar{X}_i/(1 - \lambda_i\bar{X}_i)$$

subject to the constraint that $\lambda_1 + \ldots + \lambda_n = \lambda$. This minimization problem can be solved by the use of Lagrange multipliers (Spiegel (1963)). The optimal solution must satisfy the conditions $\partial L/\partial\lambda_i = 0$, $i = 1, \ldots, n$, where

$$L = \sum_{i=1}^{n} (\lambda_i/\lambda)\, \bar{X}_i/(1 - \lambda_i\bar{X}_i) - M(\lambda_1 + \ldots + \lambda_n - \lambda)$$

and M is the Lagrange multiplier. Carrying out the differentiation, we obtain the necessary condition for optimal balancing:

$$\frac{1 - \lambda_i\bar{X}_i}{\sqrt{(\bar{X}_i)}} = K, \qquad (13.4.1)$$

where K is a constant and equals $\sqrt{1/M\lambda}$; it can be determined from the constraint $\lambda_1 + \ldots + \lambda_n = \lambda$, after expressing λ_i as a function of K from (13.4.1). This gives

$$K = \left\{ \left[\sum_{j=i}^{n} 1/\bar{X}_j - \lambda \right] \middle/ \sum_{j=1}^{n} 1/\sqrt{(\bar{X}_j)} \right\}.$$

Substituting this back into (13.4.1), we obtain

$$\lambda_i = 1/\bar{X}_i - [1/\sqrt{(\bar{X}_i)}] \left\{ \left[\sum_{j=i}^{n} 1/\bar{X}_j - \lambda \right] \middle/ \sum_{j=1}^{n} 1/\sqrt{(\bar{X}_j)} \right\} \qquad (13.4.2)$$

It is possible that for some i, $\lambda_i \leq 0$, which physically means that the ith device should not be used. This phenomenon is known as *device dropout* (Chen (1973)), and its intuitive reasonableness can be seen in the following example.

Example 13.1 Consider two devices having similar processing functions with respective average processing times of 10 milliseconds and 10 seconds. If the traffic is sufficiently light, then the fast device alone is capable of handling the entire traffic stream efficiently without needing to involve the slow device. Indeed the use of the slow device is not recommended since under light traffic there is unlikely to be much queueing, so that its processing time, which is excessive in comparison with the fast one, is in most cases be the same as its response time. In this case, the slow device should be effectively precluded from being used. A quantitative illustration of these ideas is given in the next example. □

If, in optimally balancing the load, device dropout is present, then the corresponding solution as given by (13.4.2) may not be optimal, since the recommended traffic setting is not physically realizable. In this case, we need to recompute (13.4.2) for a situation in which the non-positive values of λ_i are excluded from consideration right from the start of the optimization calculations. The following example illustrates this procedure.

Example 13.2   Three devices are available to process a Poisson stream of requests with rate $\lambda = 0.5$ request/second. The respective processing times are 1, 4, and 9 seconds. Assuming the processing times are exponentially distributed, determine the optimal load balancing conditions for this situation.

Solution   Here, we have $\lambda = 0.5$, $\bar{X}_1 = 1$, $\bar{X}_2 = 4$, $\bar{X}_1 = 9$. From (13.4.2) we obtain $\lambda_1 = 0.53$, $\lambda_2 = 0.015$, $\lambda_3 = -0.05$. This suggests that device 3 should not be used. Ignoring device 3, and re-applying (13.4.2) just for devices 1 and 2, we obtain $\lambda_1 = 0.5$, and $\lambda_2 = 0$. This suggests that the optimal setting is to route all traffic to device 1, with devices 2 and 3 dropped out of service. $\square$

13.5   Summary

In this chapter, we have outlined a number of areas in which performance problems may arise, and we have provided suggestions for effecting improvement without needing to upgrade the hardware facilities. Some of the common performance problems stem from poor parallelism, high system overhead, and low resource utilization. Possible solutions to these problems include adjusting the degree of multiprogramming, giving preferential treatment to active elements (e.g. appropriately fixing the active routines and active data portion in main memory), spreading activity across devices (e.g. through load balancing), and tailoring specific algorithms to match the behaviour and characteristics of the underlying mechanisms. These solutions may be effectively applied to improving the performance of the overall computer system, the scheduling and execution of programs, and the efficient deployment of resources.

13.6   Exercises

1.   What are the general performance problems associated with computer systems operation? Discuss to what extent the degree of multiprogramming may influence performance efficiency in this context.
2.   Explain carefully what is meant by spatial locality in program referencing. What are the possible reasons for this phenomenon?
3.   Explain carefully what is meant by temporal locality in program referencing. What are the possible reasons for this phenomenon?
4.   Two devices are available to process a Poisson stream of requests with rate $\lambda = 0.5$ request/second. The respective average processing times are 4

and 8 seconds. Determine the optimal load balancing conditions for this situation, assuming the processing times are exponentially distributed.

5. Consider n identical devices employed to process a Poisson traffic stream. What is the optimal load distribution for this situation? Comment on the intuitive reasonableness of this mathematical result.

CHAPTER 14

System Simulation

14.1 Introduction

If we wish to study the detailed properties and behaviour of a computer system exactly, then we frequently have to resort to simulation, as the analytic approach is not always adequate. For instance, even for a relatively uncomplicated system like the G/G/1, the analytic approach fails to deliver even the mean response time, and for the still simpler case M/G/1 very little is known concerning the distribution of the response time. In situations where analytic methods fail to deliver the results, an alternative then is to *observe and measure* either an actual system or a model of the system. Measuring the performance of an actual system may not be feasible because

(1) the system does not yet exist;
(2) it is wished to gauge system performance when the system is subject to different traffic and workload conditions;
(3) the system could be affected by a number of extraneous factors which cannot easily be eliminated.

It is thus often preferable to carry out the observation on a model of the system than on an actual system. Simulation consists of representing and constructing a model of the system under study by means of computer programs, and by running these programs the dynamic behaviour of the system is acted out so that by observing its development within the computer, the relevant properties of the system may be extracted.

A key activity of simulation is the generation of random numbers which are employed to characterize the statistical variations of appropriate random quantities. Random numbers may be generated when they are needed by invoking a *random number generator*, which is a computational algorithm for producing random numbers within a range of values, or they may be obtained by looking up a table of random numbers which have been previously generated by means of some random mechanism or a random number generator. Most random numbers tend to be presented within the standardized range of [0,1). The following example illustrates the basic ideas of simulation.

Example 14.1 Consider the system G/G/1 where the inter-arrival time is uniformly distributed between 0 and 10 seconds and the service time is

Table14.1

Job	Arrival (clock time)	Service requirement	Departure (clock time)	Response time
1	0	10	10	10
2	7	8	18	11
3	11	16	34	23
4	20	6	40	20
5	26	10	50	24

uniformly distributed between 0 and 20 seconds. Determine the mean response time of the system for the first 30 seconds of its operation.

Solution. Supposing by looking up a table of random numbers we obtain the following sequence of 9 random numbers {0.7, 0.4, 0.9, 0.6, 0.5, 0.4, 0.8, 0.3, 0.5}. Using the first four to generate the inter-arrival times by multiplying them by 10 then we obtain the sequence of inter-arrival times {7,4,9,6}. Likewise using the last five to generate the service times by multiplying them by 20, we obtain the sequence of service times {10, 8, 16, 6, 10}. From these random numbers we can construct Table 14.1. The response time is of course the difference between the departure and arrival times. From the last column of the table, we can compute the mean response time, which is

$$(10 + 11 + 23 + 20 + 24)/5 = 17.6 \text{ seconds.}$$

We also observe that the system is never idle after the arrival of the first job. □

In the above example, what we have done was to carry out a manual simulation making use of random numbers. We have only computed the mean response time there, but equally we could have computed the variance or even plotted the entire distribution of the response time. Had we performed the simulation on a computer, then all these quantities could have been obtained with little difficulty. In principle, of course, provided we have a sufficient supply of random numbers, we could carry out any simulations manually, but it is likely to be time consuming and inefficient. Since simulation is able to produce numerical solutions to problems, it may be regarded as a numerical problem-solving technique. Apart from providing solutions to problems which are analytically intractable, simulation can be used to test or validate a solution or theory. For example, supposing a new formula for, say, the mean response time of a queueing system has been discovered, then how does one know that the formula is correct—bearing in mind that it is not at all difficult to make a mistake in probability reasoning? In such a situation, a simulation study helps to 'debug' or 'reveal' any possible flaws in the analytic

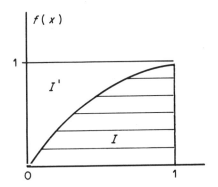

FIGURE 14.1. The Monte Carlo method

arguments leading to the formula. Likewise, in the case of conjectures or approximate solutions, a simulation study can help to ascertain their degree of accuracy. Sometimes, the term *Monte Carlo method* is used to describe simulation, but strictly speaking Monte Carlo methods are related to the solution of an inherently deterministic problem by the use of random numbers. The following is a well-known example of the application of the Monte Carlo method.

Example 14.2 (Monte Carlo Method) Given a function where $0 \leq f(x) \leq 1$, evaluate the integral

$$I = \int_0^1 f(x)\, dx.$$

Solution. It is clear that this problem is a deterministic one and the required integral corresponds to the shaded area, which occupies I units in Fig. 14.1; the size of the unshaded area is denoted by $I' = 1 - I$. Supposing we generate a pair of random numbers uniformly distributed over the interval $[0, 1)$, then the pair may be regarded as a random coordinate in the unit square in Fig. 14.1, and the probability that it falls on the shaded area, by virtue of uniformity, is simply $I/(I + I') = I$. Thus, in interpreting probability as relative frequency, we may estimate I by

$$\frac{\text{Number of random coordinates falling on shaded area}}{\text{Total number of random coordinates generated}}.$$

We note that there are more efficient methods of evaluating this particular one-dimension integral such as Simpson's rule, but the Monte Carlo method is often used in multi-dimension integration. $\square$

14.2 Random Number Generation

In producing a random number sequence of integers $\{Z_i\}$ over a given range, say, 0 to m, it is necessary to take into account the following considerations:

(1) The numbers should be uniform over the range concerned without any bias.
(2) The numbers should be independent.
(3) The numbers should be dense over the range; i.e. the generation mechanism should be able to produce a large number of distinct numbers within the given range.
(4) The underlying algorithm should be efficient.

The most widely used generator has the form of a Markov sequence

$$Z_i \equiv aZ_{i-1} + c \quad (\text{mod } m) \qquad i = 1, 2, \ldots,$$

where Z_0 is the initial number or *seed*, and such generators are often called *linear congruential generators*. Once we know the constants a, c and m we can determine the whole sequence from Z_0; more precisely, it can be shown by induction on n that

$$Z_n \equiv a^n Z_0 + c(a^n - 1)/(a - 1) \quad (\text{mod } m).$$

When $c = 0$, we call it *multiplicative congruential*, otherwise we call it *mixed congruential* (both of these being linear congruential). Since $Z_i < m$, numbers in the unit interval $[0, 1)$ can be obtained by

$$U_i = Z_i/m.$$

It is also clear that the sequence $\{Z_i\}$ can only contain at most m distinct numbers and also, as soon as any number is repeated, the entire sequence is repeated; because of such repetition, these are sometimes referred to as *pseudo-random numbers*, and the number of distinct numbers generated is called a *cycle*. To ensure that a sufficiently large number of distinct numbers are generated, we therefore wish to choose m as large as practically possible, and we also wish to select the parameters a, c and Z_0 so that as many as possible of the m numbers occur in a cycle. For a given random number generator, if p is the total number of distinct numbers in a cycle, then we say that the generator has *full period* if $p = m$. More precisely, a sequence $\{Z_i\}$ is said to have period p if p is the smallest integer such that $Z_{n+p} \equiv Z_n \,(\text{mod } m)$. Very frequently we choose m to be a power of 2 (i.e. $m = 2^b$, where b is a positive integer), so as to make computation more efficient: finding remainder and division can be accomplished simply by shifting the binary point.

Example 14.3 (A Multiplicative Congruential Generator) Here, we take $c = 0$. Letting $a = 5$, $m = 32$, $Z_0 = 2$, we obtain the sequence

$$\{2, 10, 18, 26, 2, 10, 18, 26, 2, \ldots\}.$$

We note that this sequence repeats itself after 4 integers, so that $p = 4$. If we choose $Z_0 = 7$, the resultant sequence is:

$$\{7, 3, 15, 11, 23, 19, 31, 27, 7, 3, \ldots\}$$

and we have $p = 8$. Next, if we let $a = 3$, $m = 19$, $Z_0 = 1$, then we have the sequence:

$$\{1, 3, 9, 8, 5, 15, 7, 2, 6, 18, 16, 10, 11, 14, 4, 12, 17, 13, 1, 3, \ldots\}$$

giving a significantly longer period of $p = 18$. □

It can be shown that the mixed congruential generator has full period if the following conditions hold

(1) c is relatively prime to m (i.e. the highest common factor of c and m is unity)
(2) $a \equiv 1 \pmod{q}$ for each prime factor q of m
(3) $a \equiv 1 \pmod{4}$ if 4 is a factor of m.

If we select $m = 2^b$, where b is an integer, then the first condition requires c to be odd; the second condition requires $a \equiv 1 \pmod 2$, implying the form $a = 1 + 2K$, where K is an integer; the third condition requires the form $a = 1 + 4K$, under which the previous form is already subsumed. If we take $K = 2^k$, k being an integer, then $a = 1 + 2^{k+2}$, then the operation aZ_{i-1} can be computed by shifting the binary point $k + 2$ places to the right and then adding on the original number (thus avoiding a multiplication). But how to choose the number a? It can be shown that (Greenberger (1961)) the serial correlation between the numbers U_i and U_{i+1} over the unit interval $[0, 1)$ asymptotically lies within the range

$$1/a - 6c(1 - c/m)/(am) \pm a/m.$$

One way to choose a is to minimize the upper bound of the above range. Differentiation and setting the result to zero yields $a = \sqrt{[m - 6c(1 - c/m)]}$. For $m \gg c$, which is often the case, then this is approximately $\sqrt{m}$. Thus a may be chosen so that it is roughly $\sqrt{m}$.

It is possible to modify the foregoing method to more general generators of the form (where N denotes a suitable positive integer)

$$Z_{N+n} \equiv a_0 Z_n + \ldots + a_r Z_{n+r} \pmod{m}.$$

Such a generator is known as an *additive congruential generator*; it requires a total of r initial numbers, and the associated computation is more time consuming. However, it is often able to produce better sequences in the sense of having longer periods.

Example 14.4. (Fibonacci generator)   The Fibonacci generator has the form

$$Z_{n+2} \equiv Z_{n+1} + Z_n \qquad (\text{mod } 2).$$

Here, we need to provide two initial numbers. Suppose these are $0, 1$; then we have the sequence:

$$0, 1|1, 0|1, 1|0, 1|1, 0| \ldots |0, 1|1, 0|1, 1|0, 1|, \ldots,$$

where we have grouped the sequence into doublets for legibility. Here, we are not too worried by the repetition of a single number, but when there is repetition of a doublet, then the whole sequence is repeated. The total possible number of different doublets formed from the symbols $0, 1$ is four. We remark that if the initial numbers are $0, 0$ then the sequence is not very interesting and so one normally excludes the doublet $0, 0$.   □

14.3   Generation of Continuous Non-uniform Random Numbers

A random number generator delivers random numbers uniformly distributed over the unit interval $[0, 1)$. What about more general random numbers such as those uniformly distributed over an arbitrary interval or those distributed according to a given cumulative distribution function? From random numbers uniformly distributed on $[0, 1)$, it is straightforward to generate the former as illustrated in the following example.

Example 14.5. (Uniform random numbers over an arbitrary interval)
Suppose we wish to generate a random number V uniformly distributed in the interval $[L, L')$. Then from a random number U uniformly distributed on $[0, 1)$, V can be obtained by suitably rescaling the unit interval and shifting the origin; i.e. $V = L + U(L' - L)$.   □

To generate random numbers following arbitrary distributions, we shall discuss the inverse transform method and the rejection method.

14.3.1   *Inverse Transform Method*

Suppose we wish to generate a random number conforming to a given cumulative distribution function $F(.)$. Then from a random number U uniformly distributed on $[0, 1)$, the required random number V may be obtained by setting

$$V = F^{-1}(U),$$

where F^{-1} is the inverse function of $F(.)$. Denoting the density function corresponding to $F(.)$ by $f(.)$, it is not difficult to show that V indeed conforms to the given distribution characteristics; it is so because

$$\Pr[x \leq V \leq x + dx]$$
$$= \Pr[F(x) \leq U \leq F(x + dx)]$$
$$= F(x + dx) - F(x)$$
$$\simeq f(x)\, dx.$$

The first equality is valid because $F(.)$ is a non-decreasing function. Thus we have $\Pr[x \leq V \leq x + dx] \simeq f(x)\, dx$ as required.

Example 14.6 (Generation of exponentially distributed random numbers)
Suppose

$$F(x) = 1 - \exp(-\lambda x).$$

Then

$$U = 1 - \exp(-\lambda V),$$

which implies

$$V = -[\ln(1 - U)]/\lambda.$$

But since by symmetry U and $1 - U$ are statistically indistinguishable, they have the same distribution. We thus have the following formula for generating V from U:

$$V = -[\ln U]/\lambda. \quad \square$$

14.3.2 *Rejection Method*

This method is applicable when the probability density $f(x)$ is positive over a finite interval and is bounded; i.e. there are constants a, b, and C such that

$$|f(x)| < C$$

and $\qquad f(x) > 0$ only when $a < x < b$.

In this case, the rejection method involves the following steps:

(1) generate two uniform random numbers U_1 and U_2 over the unit interval;
(2) form $V = a + (b - a)U_1$;
(3) accept V as the required random number if $U_2 \leq f(V)/C$;
(4) otherwise reject V and repeat these steps for a new pair of uniform random numbers.

In order to maximize the chance of acceptance as specified in (3), the constant C should thus be chosen to be as small as possible.

We shall omit the formal justification for this method, which may be found in Fishman (1973). Informally, its reasonableness can be seen as follows.

158

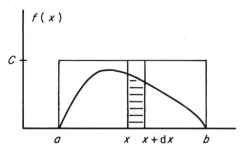

FIGURE 14.2.   The rejection method

Intuitively, we see from Figure 14.2 that

Pr[a generated number V lying between x and $x + dx$ is accepted]

$\propto$ shaded area.

The shaded area is, of course, approximately $f(x)\,dx$. Since $f(x)\,dx$ measures the likelihood of having a number lying between x and $x + dx$ drawn from the probability density $f(.)$, by accepting $V = x$, this procedure thus ensures that its value x is governed by the probability density function at that point.

14.3.3   *Generation of Normally Distributed Random Numbers*

The most intuitive approach in generating these numbers is to make use of the central limit theorem by first generating a large sequence of independent, identically distributed random numbers, and then adding them together to form the result. This method is not efficient, however, as it takes quite a few random numbers to produce the required one. A much more efficient way is to generate two random numbers U_1 and U_2 which are uniformly distributed over the unit interval $[0, 1)$, and then form

$$V_1 = \sqrt{-2 \ln U_1}\, \cos(2\pi U_2),$$
$$V_2 = \sqrt{-2 \ln U_1}\, \sin(2\pi U_2).$$

It can be shown that (see Fishman (1973)) V_1 and V_2 are independent samples from the standard normal distribution. In this way, we obtain two normally distributed random numbers from two uniformly distributed random numbers, and is therefore much more efficient than applying the central limit theorem.

14.4   Simulation Programming

In computer systems analysis, the type of simulation one normally encounters is *discrete event simulation*, which corresponds to a situation where changes to the system under study take place at discrete moments in time. This is different from *continuous system simulation* where changes can take place continuously in time, such as the simulation of the velocity of an aircraft. In discrete event simulation, there are three main approaches:

(1) event scheduling, which focuses on a detailed description of the steps that occur when an individual event takes place
(2) activity scanning, which reviews all activities to determine which can begin or terminate each time an event occurs
(3) process interaction, which follows the progress of an entity (e.g. customer) through the system from its arrival to departure.

Here, we shall be mostly concerned with the event scheduling approach. For the other approaches, please see Fishman (1973).

Since simulation is mostly concerned with the evolution of a system over time, time control in a simulation program is of vital importance. A clock is generally kept in the program, and time advancement can be of two types:

(1) when time advancement is uniform, e.g. after every second, this is called *synchronous timing*,
(2) when time advancement is variable and often oriented towards the next event (thus skipping the intermediate 'dead' time), it is called *asynchronous timing*.

Here, we shall mostly be concerned with the latter as it is more widely used in computer systems analysis. The clock time unit used in the simulation often bears little relation with the actual computer time used for the simulation—it all depends on how often you update the clock in your program. For example, in simulating a petrol station, an hour's simulation could correspond to weeks of operation, but in operating system simulation, an hour's simulation could correspond to only a few minutes of system operation. In asynchronous timing simulation, a list of events ordered in time called an *event list* or *calendar queue* is kept, and is often maintained as a list structure in memory during the simulation. In asynchronous timing simulation, we typically have the following simulation algorithm:

(1) determine the next potential event;
(2) update clock to the next event time;
(3) test whether the event can be carried out by checking various system conditions;
(4) execute event and change records in appropriate data structures;
(5) collect statistics;
(6) replenish event if applicable.

In synchronous timing simulation, the procedure is similar except that time is incremented in fixed steps, followed by checking which events can be executed at that time, and then the execution of the appropriate events.

The use of linked lists is common in simulation programming. We have already mentioned the event list. For queueing simulation, a job table is used in addition for managing the queue and the scheduling of jobs. It, too, is normally implemented as a linked list with different items on it sequenced according to the order in which the jobs are removed from the queue for service. For the event list, however, the sequencing is usually maintained in chronological order. Lists are widely used in simulation programming because they allow flexible insertion and deletion of items.

14.5 Summary

In simulation studies, the use of uniformly distributed random numbers over the interval $[0, 1)$ is almost always necessary. A common method of producing a stream of such random numbers is to make use of a random number generator to compute them when they are required in the course of the simulation. The linear congruential method of generating uniform random numbers is widely used, which makes use of an initial seed to produce a random number sequence in such a way that the next number in the sequence is determined uniquely by the current number.

Non-uniform random numbers distributed over an arbitrary interval may be obtained from uniform random numbers; two methods—the inverse transform and rejection methods—have been described for doing this. In discrete event simulation, the event scheduling approach is frequently used, which focuses attention on a detailed description of the steps that occur when an individual event takes place. The use of a clock and calendar queue is central to discrete event simulation; the algorithms and data structures used in simulation programming have also been described.

14.6 Exercises

1. Use the Monte Carlo method to determine the following integrals:

$$\int_0^1 x \, dx, \qquad \int_0^1 (1 - x) \, dx, \qquad \int_0^1 x^2 \, dx,$$

by using a sequence of 100 random numbers.

2. Determine the integrals in Exercise 1 by exact calculation and discuss the errors introduced by the Monte-Carlo method when (a) 50, (b) 100, (c) 250, and (d) 500 random numbers are used.

3. Determine the period of a multiplicative congruential generator with $a = 10$, $m = 59$, and

$$\text{(a) } Z_0 = 3, \qquad \text{(b) } Z_0 = 4, \qquad \text{(c) } Z_0 = 7,$$

and comment on the result.

4. Generate a sequence of exponentially distributed random numbers using the algorithm of Example 14.6, and make a graphical comparison between the distribution of these numbers with the theoretical curve.

5. With the help of practical examples, discuss the relationship between the simulated time in a problem and the computer time used for carrying out the simulation.

Bibliography

Abate, J. and Dubner, H. Optimizing the performance of a drum-like storage. *IEEE Trans. Computers* **C-18** (1969), 992–997.

Adams, C., Gelenbe, E. and Vicard, J. An experimentally validated model of the paging drum. *Acta Informatica* **11** (1979), 103–117.

Bard, Y. A model of shared DASD and multipathing. *Comm. ACM* **23** (1980), 564–572.

Baskett, F., Chandy, K., Muntz, R. and Palacios, F.G. Open, closed and mixed networks of queues with different classes of customers. *J. ACM* **22** (1975), 248–260.

Batory, D.S. Optimal file designs and reorganisation points. *ACM Trans. Database Syst.* **7** (1982), 60–81.

Beizer, B. *Micro-analysis of Computer System Performance*. Van Nostrand Reinhold, N.Y. (1978).

Burke, P.J. The output of a queueing system. *Opns. Res.* **4** (1956), 699–704.

Buzen, J. Analysis of system bottlenecks using a queueing network model. *Proc. ACM-SIGOPS Workshop on System Performance Evaluation* (1971), 82–103.

Buzen, J. Fundamental operational laws of computer system performance. *Acta Informatica* **7** (1976), 167–182.

Chen, P.P.S. Optimal partitioning of input load to parallel exponential servers. *Proc. 5th Annual Southeastern Symposium on System Theory*, North Carolina State University, N.C. (1973).

Coffman, E.G. Analysis of a drum input/output queue under scheduled operation in a paged computer system. *J. ACM* **16** (1969), 73–90.

Coffman, E.G. and Denning, P.J. *Operating Systems Theory*. Prentice-Hall, N.J. (1973).

Coffman, E.G. and Hofri, M. A class of FIFO queues arising in computer systems. *Opns. Res.* **26** (1978), 864–880.

Conolly, B.W. and Choo, Q.H. The waiting time process for a generalized correlated queue with exponential demand and service. *SIAM J. Appl. Math.* **37** (1979), 263–275.

Cooper, R.B. *Introduction to Queueing Theory*. Macmillan, N.Y. (1972).

Courtois, P. Decomposability, instabilities, and saturation in multiprogramming systems. *Comm. ACM* **18** (1975), 371–376.

Cox, D.R. and Isham, V. *Point Processes*. Chapman and Hall, London (1980).

Cox, D.R. and Smith, W.L. *Queues*. Chapman and Hall, London (1961).

Denning, P. The working set model for program behavior. *Comm. ACM* **11** (1968), 323–333.

Denning, P. Virtual memory. *Comp. Surv.* **2** (1970), 153–189.

Denning, P. A note on paging drum efficiency. *Comp. Surv.* **3** (1972), 1–3.

Denning, P. and Buzen, J. The operational analysis of queueing network models. *Comp. Surv.* **10** (1978), 225–261.

Drummond, M.E. *Evaluation and Measurement Techniques for Digital Computer Systems*. Prentice-Hall, N.J. (1973).

Feller, W. *An Introduction to Probability Theory and its Applications*, Vol. I (3rd edn), Wiley, N.Y. (1968).

Ferrari, D. *Computer Systems Performance Evaluation.* Prentice-Hall, N.J. (1978).

Fishman, G.S. *Concepts and Methods in Discrete Event Digital Simulation.* Wiley, N.Y. (1973).

Flynn, M.J. Trends and problems in computer organizations. *Information Processing* **74**, North-Holland, Amsterdam (1974), 3–10.

Freiberger, W. (ed.) *Statistical Computer Performance Evaluation.* Academic Press, N.Y. (1972).

Fuller, S.H. *Analysis of Drum and Disk Storage Units*, Springer-Verlag, Berlin (1975).

Gelenbe, E. and Iasnogorodski, R. A queue with server of walking type (autonomous service). *Ann. Inst. Henri Poincaré* **B-16** (1980), 63–73.

Gelenbe, E., Lenfant, J. and Potier, D. Response time of a fixed-head disk to transfers of variable length. *SIAM J. Comput.* **4** (1975), 461–473.

Gelenbe, E. and Mitrani, I. *Analysis and Synthesis of Computer Systems.* Academic Press, N.Y. (1980).

Greenberger, M. An *a priori* determination of serial correlation in computer generated random numbers. *Math. Comp.* **15** (1961), 383–389.

Gordon, G. *System Simulation* (2nd edn). Prentice-Hall, N.J. (1978).

Gordon, W.J. and Newell, G.F. Closed queueing systems with exponential servers. *Opns. Res.* **15** (1967), 254–265.

Gross, D. and Harris, C. *Fundamentals of Queueing Theory.* Wiley, N.Y. (1974).

Hellerman, H. and Conroy, T. *Computer Systems Performance.* McGraw-Hill, N.Y. (1975).

Heyman, D.P. Mathematical models of database degradation. *ACM Trans. Database Syst.* **7** (1982), 615–631.

IBM. *Introduction to IBM Direct-Access Storage Devices and Organisation Methods.* Order No. GA26-1592-4 (1976).

Jackson, J.R. Job-shop like queueing systems. *Management Sci.* **10** (1963), 131–142.

Jewell, W.S. A simple proof of $L = \lambda W$. *Opns. Res.* **15** (1967), 1109–1116.

Kendall, M. and Stuart, A. *The Advanced Theory of Statistics*, Vol. I (3rd edn). Griffin, London (1969).

Khintchine, A.Y. *Mathematical Methods in the Theory of Queueing.* Griffin, London (1960).

Kleinrock, L. Analysis of a time-shared processor. *Nav. Res. Log. Quart.* **11** (1964), 59–73.

Kleinrock, L. Time-shared system: a theoretical treatment. *J. ACM* **14** (1967), 242–267.

Kleinrock, L. *Queueing Systems*, Vol. I. John Wiley, N.Y. (1975).

Kleinrock, L. *Queueing Systems*, Vol. II. John Wiley, N.Y. (1976).

Knight, K.E. Evolving computer performance, 1962–1967. *Datamation* **14** (1968), 31–35.

Knuth, D. *The Art of Computer Programming*, Vol. I: *Fundamental Algorithms* (2nd edn). Addison-Wesley, Reading, Mass. (1973).

Knuth, D. *The Art of Computer Programming*, Vol. II: *Seminumerical Algorithms* (2nd edn). Addison-Wesley, Reading, Mass. (1981).

Knuth, D. *The Art of Computer Programming*, Vol. III: *Sorting and Searching.* Addison-Wesley, Reading, Mass. (1973).

Kobayashi, H. Application of the diffusion approximation to queueing networks—I: Equilibrium queue distributions. *J. ACM* **21** (1974a), 316–328.

Kobayashi, H. Application of the diffusion approximation to queueing networks—II: Nonequilibrium distributions and applications to computer modeling. *J. ACM* **21** (1974b), 459–469.

Kobayashi, H. *Modeling and Analysis: An Introduction to System Performance Evaluation Methodology*. Addison-Wesley, Reading, Mass. (1978).

Larson, P. Analysis of index-sequential files with overflow chaining. *ACM Trans. Database Syst.* **6** (1981), 671–680.

Lavenberg, S. (ed.) Computer Performance Modelling Handbook. Academic Press, N.Y. (1983).

Lazowska, Z., Zahorjan, J., Graham, G. and Sevcik, K. *Quantitative System Performance*. Prentice-Hall, N.J. (1984).

Leung, C.H.C. A simple model for the performance analysis of disc storage fragmentation. *Computer J.* **25** (1982a), 193–198.

Leung, C.H.C. An improved optimal-fit procedure for dynamic storage allocation. *Computer J.* (1982b), 199–206.

Leung, C.H.C. Analysis of secondary storage fragmentation. *IEEE Trans. Software Eng.* **SE-9** (1983a), 87–93.

Leung, C.H.C. Analysis of disc fragmentation using Markov chains. *Computer J.* **26** (1983b), 113–116.

Leung, C.H.C. A model for disc locality referencing. *Computer J.* **26** (1983c), 196–198.

Leung, C.H.C. Dynamic storage fragmentation and file deterioration. *IEEE Trans. Software Eng.* **SE-12** (1986), 436–441.

Leung, C.H.C. Analysis of space allocation in a generally fragmented linear store. *Acta Informatica* **24** (1987), 93–104.

Leung, C.H.C. and Choo, Q.H. The effect of fixed-length record implementation on file system response. *Acta Informatica* **17** (1982), 399–409.

Leung, C.H.C. and Choo, Q.H. On the execution of large batch programs in unreliable computing systems. *IEEE Trans. Software Eng.* **SE-10** (1984a), 444–450.

Leung, C.H.C. and Choo, Q.H. The paging drum queue: a uniform perspective and further results. *Acta Informatica* **21** (1984b), 485–500.

Leung, C.H.C. and Wolfenden, K. Disc database efficiency: a scheme for detailed assessment based on semi-Markov models. *Computer J.* **26** (1983), 10–14.

Leung, C.H.C. and Wolfenden, K. Mathematical models of file growth. *Computer J.* **28** (1985a), 179–183.

Leung, C.H.C. and Wolfenden, K. Estimating data access patterns via diffusion models. *Computer J.* **28** (1985b), 409–411.

Leung, C.H.C. and Wolfenden, K. Analysis and optimization of data currency and consistency in replicated distributed databases. *Computer J.* **28** (1985c), 518–523.

Leung, C.H.C. and Wong, K.S. File processing efficiency on the content addressable file store. *Proc. 11th International Conference on Very Large Data Bases*, Stockholm (1985), 282–291.

Lindley, D. and Miller, J. *Cambridge Elementary Statistical Tables*. Cambridge University Press (1953).

Little, J.D.C. A proof of the queueing formula $L = \lambda W$. *Opns. Res.* **9** (1961), 383–387.

Lohman, G.M. and Muckstadt, J.A. Optimal policy for batch operations: backup, checkpointing, reorganization, and updating. *ACM Trans. Database Syst.* **2** (1977), 209–222.

Maruyama, K. and Smith, S.E. Optimal reorganization of distributed space disk files. *Comm. ACM* **19** (1976), 634–642.

Mendelson, H. and Yechiali, W. Optimal policies for data base reorganization. *Opns. Res.* **29** (1981), 23–26.

Newell, G. *Applications of Queueing Theory*. Chapman and Hall, London (1971).

Oney, W. Queueing analysis of the SCAN policy for moving head disks. *J. ACM* **22** (1975), 397–412.

165

Phipps, T.E. Machine repair as a priority waiting-line problem. *Opns. Res.* **9** (1961), 732–742.
Ramirez, R.J., Tompa, F.W. and Munro, J.I. Optimum reorganization points for arbitrary database cost. *Acta Informatica* **18** (1982), 17–30.
Sauer, C.H. and Chandy, K.M. *Computer Systems Performance Modeling*. Prentice-Hall, N.J. (1981).
Shneiderman, B. Optimum data base reorganization points. *Comm. ACM* **18** (1973), 362–365.
Skinner, C.E. A priority queueing system with server-walking time. *Opns. Res.* **15** (1967), 278–285.
Spiegel, M. *Advanced Calculus*. McGraw-Hill, N.Y. (1963).
Stone, H.S. (ed.) *Introduction to Computer Architecture* (2nd ed.). Science Research Associates, Chicago (1980).
Svobodova, L. *Computer Performance Measurement and Evaluation Methods: Analysis and Applications*. American Elsevier, N.Y. (1976).
Tanenbaum, A. *Computer Networks*. Prentice-Hall, N.J. (1981).
Teorey, T.J. and Pinkerton, T.B. A comparative analysis of disk scheduling policies. *Comm. ACM* **15** (1972), 177–194.
Tuel, W.G. Optimum reorganization points for linearly growing files. *ACM Trans. Database Syst.* **3** (1978), 32–40.
van der Pool, J.A. Optimum storage allocation for a file in steady state, *IBM J. Res. Develop.* **17** (1973), 27–38.
Waters, S.J. Estimating magnetic disc seeks. *Computer J.* **18** (1975), 12–17.
Welch, P.D. On a generalised $M/G/1$ queueing process in which the first customer of each busy period receives exceptional service. *Opns. Res.* **12** (1964), 736–752.
Wiederhold, G. *Database Design* (2nd edn). McGraw-Hill, N.Y. (1983).
Wilhelm, N.C. An anomaly in disk scheduling: a comparison of FCFS and SSTF seek scheduling using an empirical model for disk accesses. *Comm. ACM* **19** (1976), 13–17.
Wilhelm, N.C. A general model for the performance of disk systems. *J. ACM* **24** (1977), 14–31.
Wong, C.K. Minimizing expected head movement in one-dimensional and two-dimensional mass storage systems. *Comp. Surv.* **12** (1980), 167–168.
Yao, S.B., Das, K.S. and Teorey, T.J. A dynamic database reorganization algorithm. *ACM Trans. Database Syst.* **1** (1976), 159–174.

INDEX

Additive congruential generator 155
Additivity 11–12, 15, 21, 22
Analytic models 1–2
Approximate solution 2
Approximations 119–23
Arrival characteristics 42–43
Arrival rate 20, 21, 42, 53, 55, 67
Arrival-to-departure ratio 72
Asynchronous timing 159
Average 10, 11

Balance equations 71, 72
Batch processing 68
Benchmarks 125
Binomial distribution 15–17, 22, 23
Bottleneck analysis 100–3
Buffer 73–75, 77, 80
Buffer allocation 32, 65
Bulk arrival 39
Burke's theorem 82–85

Calendar queue 159
Central server model 101
Channel loading 142–143
Checkpoints 146–47
Chen, P. P. S. 148
Choo, Q. H. 40, 107, 108, 111, 147
Closed queueing network 82, 90–91, 100–3
Coefficient of variation 12, 13, 18, 19, 21, 22, 24, 39, 42, 43, 47, 48, 60
Communications line 25, 31, 34, 38, 53, 67, 73, 80, 92
Complementary distribution function 9
Completely random events 16, 22
Computing power 129–31
Congestion 43
Conservative system 44–45
Contention of resources 26, 33, 142
Continuous system simulation 158
Control store 135

Cox, D. R. 56
CPU 58, 84, 92, 100–1, 112, 113, 127, 133, 135, 144
Critical workload 102
Cumulative distribution function 9, 13, 18–20, 24, 73, 110, 156
Cumulative frequency 8
Cumulative utilization 60, 61
Cyclic network 91, 93
Cyclical routing 22

Data block 73, 74, 106
Data processing centre 67
Data transfer 48
Database 40, 105–18
Database reorganization 114–18
Degenerate quantity 10, 29
Delay 35
Departure characteristics 27
Deterministic quantity 10, 29
Device dropout 148
Diffusion approximation 119, 120
Discrete event simulation 158
Discrete quantity 10
Disk locality referencing 113, 114
Disk storage unit 40
Distribution law 10
Double buffering 112, 113, 117

Effectiveness measures 32–33
Erland distribution 22
Erlang's B formula 77, 80
Erlang's C formula 77–80
Error detection and correction 25
Error-free execution 20
Error rate 20
Event-driven monitor 134
Event list 159
Evolutionary operations 144
Executable workload models 125, 126
Execution efficiency 145–47

Execution time 7, 27
Execution time interference 134
Exponential distribution 18, 19, 22–24, 29, 42, 73

Feedforward network 82, 83–86
Fibonacci generator 156
File buffering 112–14
File enquiry system 24, 48
Firmware monitor 135–36
First-in-first-out (FIFO) rule 28, 29, 35, 36, 44, 46, 49, 61–64, 67, 69, 106, 108–10
Fishman, G. S. 157, 159
Fixed head disk 41, 47, 106–9
    with fixed length records 107–9
    with variable length records 106–7, 109
    with write verification 48
Flexibility 125
Flow balance 95, 96, 98, 100
Flow balance equations 99
Flynn, M. J. 129
Forced flow law 99
Frequency function 8–11, 16, 19, 25
Frequency histogram 7
Fuller, S. H. 109

G/G/1 119–23, 151
G/G/7 123
G/G/m 119, 122
Gantt chart 136–37, 141
Gelenbe, E. 64, 83, 86, 90
General distribution 29
General response time law 100
Generalized Pollaczek–Khintchine formulae 40–42, 45, 47, 108, 111
Geometric distribution 14–15, 18, 22–24, 74, 78
Greenberger, M. 155

Hardware monitor 4, 132–33, 141
Hashing algorithm 15, 25
Heavy traffic approximation 119, 122
Histogram 7
Hybrid model 4
Hybrid monitor 135–36

Indexed files 113, 118
Inflexibility 125

Initiators 40, 41, 107, 108, 112
Input 27
Instruction mixes 127–29
Instruction time 128
Interactive response time formula 75–77
Interactive system 76, 79, 80, 96, 97, 102, 104, 130
Inter-arrival distribution 29
Inter-arrival time 19–22, 42, 43, 47
Inter-event time 22
Inter-point time interval 19
Interrupt interference 134
Interrupt processing 58
Interval-arrival time 25
Interval description 18–20
Invariance 45, 54–56
Inverse transform method 156–57, 160
I/O devices 45, 73, 100, 104, 113, 117
I/O overlap 143
I/O subsystem 105–18
I/O transfers 113

Jackson's theorem 86, 89, 92
Jewell, W. S. 36
Job completions 97

Kernels 126, 130
Khintchine, A. Y. 23
Kiviat graph 137–39, 141
Kleinrock, L. 30, 37, 55, 62, 64, 71
Knight, K. E. 130

Lagrange multiplier 148
Last-in-first-out (LIFO) rule 28, 29, 45, 49, 69
Latency 105, 106
Leung, C. H. C. 40, 107, 108, 111, 113, 114, 116, 145, 147
Linear congruential generator 154
Lists 159–60
Little's formula 35, 36, 38, 45, 51, 52, 73, 79, 85, 88, 95, 99
Load balancing 147–49
Load optimization 147–49
Locality referencing 112–14, 145
Logical filter circuit 132
Logical record 106
Loss system 27

M/D/1 43
M/G/1 29, 38, 39, 43, 44, 46, 64, 123, 151
M/G/1:CONS 45, 66
M/G/∞ 79, 80
M/M/1 29, 69, 72–75, 79, 122, 147
  with finite population 75–77
  with limited buffer 73–75
M/M/1:SJF 69
M/M/2 29
M/M/5 80
M/M/6 123
M/M/m 77–80, 82–83, 92
M/M/m_i 86
M/M/∞ 79, 80
Markov sequence 154
Maximum throughput 102, 103
Mean 10, 12–15, 17, 18, 21, 22, 24, 42, 110
Measures of effectiveness 32–33
Memory space interference 134
Memoryless property 19, 22, 29
Merging of Poisson process 20–22
Messages 25, 31, 34, 38, 53, 57, 67, 68, 73, 80, 83, 85, 87, 88, 92
Microprograms 135–36
Minimum throughput 102
Mitrani, I. 64, 83, 86, 90
Mixed congruential 154
Monitoring tools 132–36
Monte Carlo method 153, 160
Movable head disk 109–12, 117
  with fixed length records 111
  with variable length records 110–11
Multiplicative congruential generator 154, 155, 160
Multi-processor system 21, 25, 31, 77
Multiprogramming 143

Network throughput 102
Non-executable model 125
Non-initiators 40, 42, 107, 108
Non-loss system 27
Non-negative quantities 12
Non-preemptive priority 50–57, 66, 67
Normalized mean waiting time 37, 43, 44
Nth moment 11
Number of servers 29

Oney, W. 111
Open queueing network 81, 85–90

Operational analysis 94–104
Operational laws 94–97
Operational theorem 95
Operational variables 94
Optimal priority assignment 56–57
Optimization 4
Output process 82
Overflow probability 25, 65

Page replacement algorithm 143
Paging system 145
Performance improvement 142–50
Performance measurement 124, 132–41
Performance monitoring 132–41
Performance optimization 4
Performance tuning 4–5, 142–50
Phipp's formula 60, 66
Physical record 106
Point description 17–18
Point events 16–23
Poisson distribution 17, 22, 23, 79
Poisson input 27, 36, 42, 45
Poisson process 17, 20, 22, 23, 25, 38, 39, 44, 45, 47, 48, 50, 53, 55, 61, 65, 67, 69, 80, 82, 84, 85, 105, 147
Pollaczek–Khintchine formulae 37–39, 43–46, 55, 60–61, 64, 72, 73, 84, 88, 106, 107, 111, 120
Predictive evaluation 4
Preemptive priority scheduling rule 28
Preemptive resume priority systems 57–59
Preemptive rules 66
Preemptive scheduling rule 44
Priority assignment 56–57
Priority index 50, 52, 57, 58
Priority scheduling 68
Priority system 52
Probabilistic model 2
Probability 14–18, 65, 71, 86, 88–90
Probability density 22, 107, 110
Probability density function 8, 10, 16, 18, 23, 60
Probability mass function 9, 10, 11, 14, 16, 23, 24
Probability statement 6
Processing time 27, 51, 148–49
Processor sharing (PS) rule 63–66
Processor utilization 65, 76
Program behaviour 145–47
Pseudo-random numbers 154

Quantum 62, 64–66, 69
Queue size 35, 120
Queueing network 23, 81–93, 97–100
Queueing system 26–28, 33, 152
  non-preemptive priority 66
Queueing theory 76

Random events 16
Random number generator 151, 154
Random numbers 152
  continuous non-uniform 156
  exponentially distributed 157, 161
  non-uniform 160
  normally distributed 158
  over arbitrary interval 156
  uniformly distributed 160
Random quantity 10–12, 22, 27
Random routing 21
Random seek distribution 109–10
Record format 106
Record transfer time 106
Reduced instruction set computers (RISCs) 128
Rejection method 157–58, 160
Relative frequency 129, 131, 153
Representative workload 124
Request arrival characteristics 26–27
Residual service delay 46, 47, 51
Resolution 133
Resource contention 26, 33, 142
Response time 32, 33, 36–42, 58, 59, 76, 84, 85, 88, 90, 97, 99, 100, 102, 107, 108, 111, 112, 147, 152
Rotational delay 48, 105, 112
Rotational latency 111
Rotational position sensing 14, 142
Round-robin (RR) rule 62–63, 65, 66, 69
Routing frequency 87, 99

Sample-driven monitor 134
Saturated system 30, 101
Scaling 125
SCAN rule 109, 111
Scheduling rule 28, 29, 32, 35, 44
Scripts 126–27
Sector 106
Seed 154
Seek characteristic 110, 111
Seek distance 109, 110
Seek time 24, 109, 112
Sequential file 23–24, 48, 112

Service capacity 27–28
Service characteristics 43–44
Service discriminations 50–69
Service distribution 29
Service rate 28, 30
Service requirement 27
Service time 24, 32, 41, 42, 46, 106–9, 112, 142, 152
Shneiderman, B. 114
Shortest-job-first (SJF) rule 44, 59–61, 69
Shortest-latency-time-first (SLTF) scheduling rule 106, 108
Simpson's rule 153
Simulation 151–61
Simulation model 2–3
Simulation programming 158–60
Smith, W. L. 57
Software monitor 4, 133–35, 141
Software probe 134
Spatial locality 145
Splitting of Poisson process 20–22
Stable system 29–30, 33
Stack processing 45
Standard deviation 11, 12, 22
Standardized benchmarks 126
State-transition-rate diagram 71
Storage management algorithms 145
Storage structures 106
Supervisor mode 143
Swapping overhead 64, 65
Synchronous timing 159
Synthetic jobs 125–26, 130
System failure 146
System-oriented measures 32
System state 70
System utilization profile 136

Tandem network 85, 92
Temporal locality 145
Think time 75
Thrashing 143, 146
Throughput 31, 32
Time-dependent system 119–23
Time-sharing system 65, 69
Traffic equations 87–89, 92
Traffic intensity 29, 31, 33, 49, 55, 56, 65, 69, 111
Transmission errors 25
Triple buffering 117
Tuning 4–5, 142–50
Turnaround time 32

Uncertainty 6
Unfinished work 66
Uniform distribution 12–14
Urgency factor 57
User-oriented measures 32
Utilization 30, 32, 34, 39, 41, 42, 44, 48,
    78, 89, 101, 107, 108, 143, 144
Utilization factor 30, 40, 62
Utilization law 95

Variance 11–13, 18, 22, 42, 110, 114,
    115, 117

Visit ratio 99, 100, 101
Visit ratio equations 99

Waiting time 32, 40, 51, 52, 55, 56, 120
Window size 146
Wolfenden, K. 113
Wong, C. K. 113
Work 29, 44
Working set 146
Workload characterization 124–31
Workload model 124–31
Write verification 48